The Leadership Shift

How to Lead Successful Transformations in the New Normal

A Practical and Guide

for

Today's Executive Leaders

by

Stuart Andrews

Absolute Author
Publishing House

Publisher: Absolute Author Publishing House

Library of Congress Catalogue-in-Publication-Data

The Leadership Shift/*Stuart Andrews*

p. cm.

Paperback ISBN: 978-1-64953-417-0

eBook ISBN: - 978-1-64953-418-7

1.   Leadership   2. Business   3. Management

Printed in the United States of America

Table of Contents

Note: This text uses Australian spelling and academic expectations. Direct quotations are taken from outside sources; however, spelling and grammar are strictly recorded as used by that author

Introduction

The pace of change is unrelenting, and customers expect more than ever before. The advent of the Internet of Things (IoT) is creating a major shift in the way products and services are traded and is poised to transform both the customer experience and the future of work. The IoT is creating an opportunity for businesses to rethink the value chain, and to understand the roles of technology, data and people.

The unabated drive toward "digital everywhere" is fuelled by news and misinformation of Artificial Intelligence (AI), Big Customer Data, Robotics, and Automation. These forces and more will transform all aspects of industry, education, economics, and sociology. They affect production, service, quality, and delivery while strategically focusing on extracting every ounce of efficiency possible to gain the edge on competitors.

The COVID-19 pandemic happened to define a *turning* into a new future where nothing remains constant. This emerging context requires Executive Leaders with vision, courage, and conviction to drive the necessary transformation and—more important—a culture to cultivate and inspire the motives that drive success.

Executive Leaders must recognise the importance of rich data while emerging technology and innovation continues as the critical enabler affecting necessary change.

All organisations change over time. They must change if they expect to survive. Change may originate internally, or it may be a response to external forces. It involves much more than a shift from point "A" to point "B." In this book, change means much more than a change of address or a switch to another internet provider. Instead, it explores the sophisticated and tricky moves that lead to, trigger, and follow growth.

Leadership—together with the organisation's people at all levels— enables and empowers transformation. Growth and success may prompt change. Shortfalls and failures both call for a defensive regrouping to rescue the organisation. Changes in markets and competition will initiate transformation which is shaped by both external governance and customer experience. Finally, powerful tools, training, and technology drive transforming transition.

Transformation evolves as a work-in-process. Consistent and continuous, fluid and flexible—the change must be dynamic and organic, with executive leadership championing and driving the design, build, and execution of organisational transformation.

Here's What to Expect

This book is an invaluable and must-read resource for both leaders and executives embarking on orchestrating Organisational Transformation and Change. Decision-makers must enter this process armed with the correct facts and expertise to ensure the achievement of successful outcomes.

The Leadership Shift offers a practical guide to leaders and executives involved in or responsible for orchestrating change and transformation.

The following four sections provide analysis, problem-solving, and relevant experiences. I have sought to provoke thought as much as to create a practical guide for execution. The work here should spur discussion and growth for everyone inside and outside the highest executive level.

- **Section 1** looks at why executives should know how to ask the right questions, believing *leaders should ask more than tell, listen more than command.*

  Listening and engaging with employees and enhancing the customer experience are critical leadership habits—habits that increase executive power and influence with an expansive information base.

- **Section 2** will focus on solving the correct problems, those specific to your organisation. These chapters clarify your individual strategy—building, framing, and mastering a value proposition *far from* and *better than* the competition.

iii

Creating, strengthening, and sustaining your leadership role also requires a discerning use of technology, that same technology that enables and drives the flow of information needs mastery. Information and analytic technology have brought rapid changes. They have made it possible to understand and approach customers while simplifying internal functional processes. However, tech acceleration tests executives and their leadership teams to select, adapt, and implement the suitable systems to serve stakeholder expectations, including customers and employees best. The risks include loss of revenue, talent, and investment, risks with irrevocable impact.

- **Section 3** encourages successful execution with the strategic use of teams. Executive Leaders should set the tone, establish alignment, and optimise operations, but they must also build employee engagement by living the organisation's core values. They should define the future of work rather than fall victim to the transformation in the nature of the work.

Executive Leaders must own technology's promise. They must leverage the emerging advanced technology that empowers employees, enables innovation, and enhances customer experience. Investor returns, customer satisfaction, and talent retention all centre on the strategic use of technology.

- **Section 4** offers direction on making this vision real. Executive Leaders face challenges of size and scale that vary across economic sectors, products, and services. Challenges like these can be complicated and unpredictable.

The final challenge may be accepting the need for external, trusted advice. Prudent leaders retain the resources, experience, and power with Trusted Advisors to identify, diffuse, and resolve these challenges.

Section 1

Chapter 1: Today's Executive Leadership Challenges

Here's What to Expect

- ✓ "Executive" defined
- ✓ Benchmark Responsibilities
- ✓ Benchmark Accountabilities
- ✓ "Leadership" defined
- ✓ Challenges posed and understood

Held to high accountability, senior executives always face challenges. Many are constructive tests of skill and character. Some disrupt and defeat. The strongest Executive Leaders *stand up to*—and *lean into*—expected and unexpected challenges.

A study published in *Harvard Business Review* found close to 50 percent of chief executives found the job was not what they expected (Kissel & Foley, 2019). This disappointment and disconnect may explain the departure of so many highly placed executives early into their tenure. Regardless of the organisation's size or the economic sector served, dissatisfied, distracted, and discouraged executives prove costly.

The challenges take many forms. They are short- and long-term concerns. There are problems inside and outside the organisation. It helps if executives prepare to manage what comes at them.

Executive Leaders and executives-in-the-works will find options, paths, and solutions in these pages; a better understanding of those expectations can make the road a more comfortable ride. The information presented is not intended to be all-inclusive; rather, it is a collection of ideas to help you find and meet your personal challenge.

A Working Definition

Defining "executive" seems simple enough: however, finding a definition that fits the person and function can be challenging. One common element is *responsibility,* but *responsibility* has given way these days to *accountability.* Understanding the difference may be the first steady step to executive leadership positions.

Executives are *responsible* for establishing strategic priorities that drive goals, frame policies, and direct processes. The focus on *accountability* shifts the emphasis to the affirmation of core values, co-collaboration with other executives, alignment of activities and decisions with corporate goals and values, and the significant contribution to social impact.

Benchmark *Responsibilities:*

The following shortlist of executive duties offers a baseline to measure individual duties and *responsibilities* for a senior executive leader:

- *Formulate, implement,* and *oversee* organisation policies on internal and external corporate behaviour to comply with agency governance, community norms, and stated core values.

- *Enable* and *empower* diversity and inclusivity at every level and in every function.

- *Represent* the organisation's interests in customer relationships, contract negotiations, media presentations, mergers and acquisitions, and other duties calling for an authoritative voice.

- *Present* the organisation's performance, concerns, and needs to the Board of Directors and investor stakeholders.

- *Direct* corporate budget and authorise financial statements.

- *Delegate* responsibilities for growth, reporting, production, and development.

Executive Leaders must *do things right*, make things happen. Responsibilities are *tasks*, lists of *actions* within the executive's position's range and scope. The measures are clear, concrete, and unequivocal.

Traditional organisation charts ("org charts") arrange positions in vertical columns (silos). The columns indicate the sequence of reporting responsibilities. The silos are descriptive; however, they can also discourage or prevent cross-functional cooperation.

Benchmark *Accountabilities:*

Accountabilities, however, flow in multiple directions. Executives have accountability to their owners and Boards of Directors. They are accountable to stockholders. More critically, executives are accountable to their employees, customers, communities, and the environment.

Corporate mission statements increasingly place the organisation in the centre of financial, social, and sustainable ecosystems. Local and global competition has prompted a paradigm shift in executive roles.

> "*The reason most people don't succeed in work or in life is that they are not accountable enough to themselves or to those whom they serve*" (Llopis, 2012).

The following shortlist of executive accountabilities offers metrics for understanding the executive *accountabilities*:

- *Promote and model* the organisation's core values.

- *Prioritise* employee wellbeing in their life/work balance, equitable compensation, benefits, and workplace environment.

- *Increase* organisation success and revenue growth within a broader context of respect for material resources, intellectual property, and customer experience.

- *Honour* investor expectations for reliable dividends, fiduciary financial management, and public image.

- *Build and support* an Executive Team that drives team values and behaviours throughout the organisation.

- *Invest* in recruiting, developing, and retaining the existing and future talent necessary for scalability and sustainability.

Executive Leaders must *do the right thing*, always deciding in favour of the enriching experience and value. Accountability is about making good choices, building trust, and supporting a learning culture. It means accepting no excuse for ownership of the organisation's success—or failure.

All about Leadership

Executive Leaders want people to respect and trust them. The greatest Executive Leaders build strong relationships and stay in touch with the concerns of others. They show excellent judgment while seeking their Trusted Advisors' opinions, and they become role models for team members.

The most effective executives are strong leaders. Responsibility and accountability must inform each other so they cannot be differentiated. Leadership skills and capabilities pull them together. The leadership thought-leader John C. Maxwell famously said, "*Leadership is not about titles, positions or flowcharts. It is about one life influencing another*" (Maxwell, 1997).

Legacy executives have driven organisations authoritatively. They confused force with decisiveness and led with authority and coercion. *Coercive* executives create bureaucracies bordered by stringent policies that lose influence over time. Entrepreneurs and executives alike have often driven their organisations into the ground with unremitting laser-like energy that demands too much of their partners, employers, and customers.

Instead, organisations need Executive Leaders with a strategic playbook to encourage innovation, improvisation, and ownership. They succeed best in collaborative environments where teams know the rules but feel empowered to act independently within their respective skill set. Team members value speed, agility, and responsiveness. They respect their peers and forge emotional connections with internal and external stakeholders.

Cultivating personal talent, taking ownership of responsibilities, and constructing an authentic leadership style—these all sit high among the challenges facing Executive Leaders today.

The Executive Leader's Situation

Executive Leaders face many challenges. Depending on whom the researchers survey, challenges vary across various industry sectors, organisation size, and socio/economic/political conditions. For example, surveys of CEOs report the following:

- 80% of CEOs have faced a financial crisis (Welcome to the crisis era, 2017).

- 70%+ "*believe they need to lead a radical digitally-led transformation of their business model*" (Thomas, 2019).

- 70% need help with talent strategy and execution (CEO Benchmarking Report, 2019).

- 80% of CEOs are concerned about regulations (Emmons, 2019).

It is not surprising then that in another study (Age and Tenure, 2017), they found CEOs hold vulnerable positions. Internal and external challenges determine their tenure and careers forcefully, challenges they can address and overcome.

Held to high accountability, Executive Leaders will always face challenges. Some challenges test skill and character. Other challenges disrupt and defeat. Nonetheless, the strongest executives will *stand up*—and *lean into*—expected and unexpected challenges.

The executives who find themselves in transition or accountable for organisational transformation face challenges that take many forms. There are short- and long-term concerns. Challenges come from inside and outside the organisation. Moreover, some executives create their own problems. It helps if they are prepared to manage what comes at them.

1. **Recruiting, developing, and retaining talent.**

Strong leaders admit they cannot lead without a broad and deep team. However, the supply and demand affecting needed talent have reached a critical pain point as organisational growth, purpose, and technology accelerate. Executive Leaders will not leave finding and recruiting talent to junior officers or functions. They will not delegate the accountability to Human Resources. Instead, Executive Leaders will actively identify, interview, and land the talents fit for their culture and strategy.

2. Defining and managing relationships.

People judge Executive Leaders by the company they keep. They must develop quality relationships inside and outside the organisation. They must build continuing solid relationships with shareholders and stakeholders. Moreover, they must form high-performance teams.

3. Focusing on what counts.

Every organisation has *pain points*. Any focus must address them quickly. However, strong leaders keep their eyes and ears wide open for new opportunities at those challenging points. Successful organisations turn these opportunities into sustained growth, innovation, and transformational change. Such opportunities require Executive Leaders with strength in discernment—the capacity for differentiating values, threats, and priorities.

4. Turning ships around.

Newly appointed leaders naturally believe they have something new to contribute. They assume they have been appointed to make things move. So, they arrive eager to make changes. Their first challenge lies in knowing *what needs to be done* as much as *what can be done,* and second, in communicating needs for stakeholders to take ownership of the change. So, Executive Leaders should prepare to be patient.

5. Solving the right problems and reducing risk.

Executive Leaders are positioned to solve problems. People expect them to remove barriers to success, reduce risks to employees, and fulfil promises made to customers. All other duties are subordinate to problem-solving. As those problems multiply and vary, leaders must demonstrate resilience, commitment, and optimism. It is their job to juggle and integrate the demands using tools and tactics to resolve the problems.

6. Leading with empathy and determination.

Stakeholders expect their leaders to lead from a position of strength. Some executives see that as their authorization to command and drive. Others succeed from a place of understanding. They appreciate what customers need now and into their future, and they enable and empower employee contributions to collaboration and innovation. They understand their executive position depends on much more than a title.

Metrics for leadership strength and courage may seem vague, but they are tangible, observable, and measurable. Consistency is the primary measure. People relish leadership that sticks to its word.

They want leadership behaviours that align with organisational goals.

Leaders should be dynamic and charismatic, but these energies must define and deliver practices that conform to shared goals and aspirations. However, "consistency" does not mean "sameness." Quite the contrary, consistent behaviours emerge and evolve to carry goals forward. These behaviours align with ethics and integrity. Such leadership attracts, engages, and sustains the talent that drives organisations to excellence.

Two Aligned Paths

The following chapters will develop themes on aligned paths. First, Executive Leaders must carry forward the passion, energy, and visionary dynamic that distinguishes entrepreneurs. Second, they must build and strengthen their tactical capabilities if they are to actualise their strategic purpose.

Consequently, you can expect a frequent emphasis here on visualisation, collaboration, and listening. The best practice for any organisation expects Executive Leaders to reach their employees and customers, linking their employee possibilities with customer expectations. Leading this transition during a volatile and uncertain climate presents challenges unique to these circumstances.

Here's Your Takeaway

It helps you navigate the challenges presented by transformational change if you know who you are. That is, you should consider where you are in the context of known and unforeseen issues.

You should look at how far you have progressed in your personal plan of action. Ask yourself:

1.   "Am I paid for my talent?"

2.   "What are my personal goals and targets?"

3.   "How many years will it take me to reach my targets?"

It also helps to open earnest conversations with family, friends, and people you respect. You should encourage them to give you frank feedback on your personal style, strengths, and needs to improve. Their inputs should expand your sense of self and your role in things.

The following chapters examine the size and risk presented by various challenges and offer solutions and best practices to learn more, build strength, and sustain your success. Even those organisations considered to be customer-centric must reach deeper to find answers to questions investors, employees, and customers ask—or have yet to ask.

Chapter 2: The Power of Data to Improve Customer Experience

Here's What to Expect

- ✓ The nature and value of Big Data
- ✓ Emerging technologies
- ✓ Finding the customer in the data
- ✓ Value of customer insights
- ✓ Identifying and managing customer expectations
- ✓ Tailoring the customer experience
- ✓ Customer-centric and agile execution

Data is the most valuable asset in today's economy. Its value to organisations about prospective or existing customers is priceless. As digitisation, social networks, and AI continue to evolve, those organisations that can piece together customer needs and opportunities will have a significant advantage.

Data governance is essential to capture and retain the value of data. The data governance process is a journey that begins with understanding the customer, their data and their requirements.

Progressive and innovative organisations work hard to create or remake internal departments, processes, and systems to capitalise on this new digital commodity.

Recently, the shift to make "easy-to-use" online self-service functions available for customers generates positive feedback. When done well, this helps achieve significant benefits, such as reduced manual processes, customer convenience, operational efficiency, and increased revenue.

However, the data generated is not "pure." That is, celebrated resources like Google, Facebook, and YouTube are *curated.* They archive data supporting their interest in remaining profitable; they sort and integrate data to serve the markets paying for their support.

Their fundamental purpose in data gathering does not lessen its sophistication and marketing value. However, the information found there has a bias.

It requires Executive Leaders to understand, value, and leverage the data that directly and indirectly affects Customer Experience (CX). Competition for customers means mining, refining, and harvesting data to engage markets and turn their interests and behaviours into action.

Here's My Story

With a history of fragmented systems architecture and associated data inconsistencies, a large multinational organisation found itself struggling to provide a 360-degree view of its customers. As a result, it found itself with an array of customer service complaints, poor experiences, and declining revenue.

A discovery process was set up to understand the pain points, overarching strategy and ambition. It became apparent there were conflicting priorities across business units and misalignment on technology strategy, complimented with budget and resource constraints. The strive for improving customer experience (CX) was at the forefront of every strategy and internal communication and yet when it came to execution, there was layers of bureaucracy and complexity.

Technology was the essential capability to help drive a single view of the customer that included the history and most importantly the latest customer interaction with the brand. Without the required technology refresh, legacy source applications & processes were continuing to drive inconsistencies in the CX.

Within the first month of engagement, a rescue program of work with the right governance, structure and cadence was set up to deliver quick wins in the overall roadmap. The importance of executive coaching and sponsorship coalition was pivotal in the success of this initiative. It was a game changer in the transformation this initiative brought about with robust capability and next generation proactive customer engagement. It put the organisation at the forefront of data analytics and shifted the needle on customer experience to levels unseen before. The brand is now one of the most valuable brands in the country.

Transformation in a digitised world takes more than accumulating and sorting numbers, statistics, and percentages. It requires systems and executive leadership able to convert that data to revenue. Systems and Executive Leaders must invest in personalised marketing and whatever it takes to push their CX to the next level, designing every move to *WOW* their potential and current customers.

Accelerating and emerging technologies have strengthened the challenges. They present many more paths for decision-making, multiplying the factors that shape the context for choices. Technology advances have complicated the decisions regarding the need for technology in specific situations and the best practice for application and execution. These multiple pressures tell Executive Leaders that they may not make such a transformation without expert support.

Executive Leaders must first remember their customers are people. Big Data on their behaviour is invaluable, but it may not reflect customer uniqueness fully. Customers have infinite idiosyncrasies. Their tastes vary and may change hour by hour. People make spontaneous decisions, and they buy impetuously. For instance, they will stop at a business because it is on the "right" side of the street on their way home. They will invest in something to keep up with a neighbour, please someone else, or simply satisfy a whim.

Business-to-Business (B2B) organisations buy differently. They monitor motives and decisions for economic and performance efficiency. They need products with defined shelf-life, and organisation purchasers want goods with demonstrated quality fit for their production and operation. They will buy from those organisations that support them with attractive packaging, inventory control, and just-in-time delivery.

Each of these touchpoints creates data. There is nothing new about that. The data's value lies ultimately in its utility. However, only evolving data systems can gather and use this information strategically.

In the past, data users measured the utility mostly in terms of its revenue potential. New approaches focus on revenue potential as an outcome of enhanced CX. For example, legacy systems accumulated data on demographics, timing, inventory turns, and cost-effectiveness.

New approaches do more with data. They seek to:

- *Customise* marketing images and collateral material to niche markets.
- *Engage* potential customers with interactive digital experiences.
- *Focus* on the competition's performance with like products in like markets or with unique products in niche areas.
- *Satisfy* customer needs to fast and secure delivery.
- *Ensure* customer cybersecurity.
- *Creates* customer service forums and communities.
- *Use* patterns to put select products on multiple channels and platforms.
- *Leverage* loyalty rewards to recognise, retain customers, and much more.

Customers present past, current, and future challenges for Executive Leaders, and it takes agile executive leadership to move among and around these challenges deftly.

Finding the Customer in the Data

Marketers have long prepared customer profiles. They draw a circle around a cluster of demographics, believing their product will appeal to people categorised by age, ethnicity, education level, gender, location, and other classes. The data available, collected, and analysed is invaluable; however, it is not inevitable. Analysts look for meaningful clusters among the seemingly infinite data bytes. Such data mining can only get close to a "*true*" customer, but evolving technology has narrowed that gap between descriptive data and predictive data.

With more finite customer profiles, the organisation can map advertising, sales presentations, collateral materials, and other approaches to customer buying needs and habits. Actually, these *customer* profiles are *consumption* profiles "*based on data obtained by the tracking of the customer's past consumption habits or the stated consumption habits as outlined by the customer himself*" (Bensemana, 2007). Integrating those past patterns and self-disclosed preferences helps companies develop a surer sense of their market.

Executive Leaders may not mine their marketing data firsthand, but they must know what is happening. They must know enough about market analysis to monitor and evaluate the marketing info presented because decision-making is their job. They must understand what the data shows about the past, what news the current data contains, and where they want those clusters to move. Executive involvement can make a difference between stakeholder satisfaction, complacent performance, or market leadership.

The Value of Customer Insights

Customers are quick to tell an organisation what they think. They will phone Customer Service to complain about a product's quality, incorrect size, damaged or late delivery, and so on. Most complainants want immediate satisfaction on their terms.

However, today's customers have more channels to voice their complaints. They will vent on multiple social media platforms, and organisations find themselves hard-pressed to keep up with and resolve the criticism.

Some organisations develop collaborative Customer Service responses, eager and equipped to satisfy customer complaints at once. Other companies have emphasised preventive measures instead of reactive modes. The strategy suggests, if the process eliminates the product faults, improved products will preclude complaints.

These strategies are effective, and Executive Leaders would be prudent to ensure both lines of thinking are functioning. However, neither approach really listens to the customer. "*The goal of traditional market research is simply to gather data about customers. But this objectifies customers and creates a dynamic of observer-observed*" (Mulqueen, 2018).

Contemporary strategies include inviting, involving, and integrating the inputs from everyone who touches the product from conception to reception. They are called *Customer Insight Communities (CIC)*.

They differ from traditional market research, focus groups, and customer feedback resources *"because they're made up of a cross-section of customers, employees, shareholders, and more – people who have a stake in your organisation in a variety of ways"* (Mulqueen, 2018). There are outside providers anxious to supply such services, or you can invest in developing your organisation's insight communities.

The lesson learned lies in the quality and diversity of the feedback. This collaborative approach *invites* all the voices involved, *enables a* discussion that is a negotiation at its core, and *embraces* messages more than data. Unlike data, messages occur in and refine a context. They inform, educate, and train, and the results revise, refine, reimagine, and reinvent products.

The many digital tools in use develop customer insights. Executive Leaders can check resources like Google Analytics, Klout, Facebook Audience Insights, Google Surveys, and more to gather and monitor customer inputs. While the patterns analysed and reported can be crucial to marketing decisions, accountable executives should look for more:

- **Act without waiting.**

  Executive Leaders must reach out to identify customer activities. They should lean into challenges and take strategic steps, positive moves that reduce after-the-fact reactions.

  "Leaning into" means getting inside customers' heads instead of waiting for their buying decisions. The reasonable and regular use of customer surveys, for example, mines individual and group data. Instead of just measuring customer satisfaction, the information reveals what products customers want, need, and imagine. Instead of just soliciting feedback, you build data you might call *feed-forward*.

- **Make a call.**

  Phone calls or in-person interviews also access customer details. Calls to would-be customers, recent customers, and loyal customers develop more marketing depth. It takes time and special training because most people naturally resist solicitation.

  However, framed and phrased correctly, a quality outreach by phone can also build relationships. Open-minded customers will appreciate the check on their satisfaction. They are only too happy to offer opinions. Moreover, making the call shows respect for their role.

  Some high-level executives call at least one customer per day. They identify themselves by their name and title with a particular interest in the market. A few questions will prompt the customer to open. The executive is not compelled to act on the customer's input, but enough calls will provide a feel for the customer's personality, adding dimension to the data.

- **Get a good look.**

  Unfortunately, most data resources lack this personal dimension. The constant gathering of numbers, transactions, dollars, and demographics builds and expands the understanding of markets. Still, you can do more.

If shopping and purchasing are behaviours, you should get close to that behaviour. For instance, if customers buy your products from retail stores, you should visit those stores and watch them. There is a benefit in mingling among customers. With eyes and ears wide open, you want to see how they interact with store displays, what size and colours they browse through, and how much space they have for your product in their shopping cart.

If your organisation sells online, you can watch the flow of transactions. You can also track the time people spend on your site, how often they opt for a cheaper product, and what they have in their online cart. For example, if customers have products in their cart but have not made the buy decision, you can alter those products' prices to motivate them. Moreover, the cart contents provide information on the customer's *wants,* helping you forecast *needs.*

Such outreach efforts initiate customer relationships that you can build into trusting customer loyalty. If your responsibilities limit your hands-on outreach, you must try to step in where it works for you and the customer. If you delegate these tasks, you must anticipate and understand the results provided in this research.

Clearly, if you can design, monitor, and evaluate your customer contribution, you will have increased your executive depth in building growth and loyalty.

Managing Customer Expectations

Executive Leaders cannot please everyone. This is not an *either/or* situation. Your organisation cannot meet some customer expectations. The organisation should not overextend itself if those expectations are unrealistic. However, your organisation should assess what is needed to meet achievable expectations.

- **Put your best face forward.**

    For decades, Customer Service units have developed without proactive accountability. They have taken customer calls and determined how to channel those complaints. That is, if the product required repairing or replacement, they would process the need. However, some Customer Service units resisted customer feedback because repair and replacement cost the organisation.

    Most companies have moved past that paradigm in favour of Customer Service teams with a level of professionalism. They impress customers with patience, active listening, and empathy. They expedite customer expectations or move the call to a higher decision level—with a smile.

    Trends see organisations creating a culture of customer professionalism where employees at every level in every function can deal with customers on a first-person level. Customers are pleased and satisfied, for instance, if they can talk directly to the Shipping & Handling office or the Chief of Operations. These personal connections go a long way to calming and soothing negative or confused customer expectations.

- **Multiply the options.**

Most customers do not plan to take advantage of the organisation, so there is no advantage in creating a defensive Customer Service. There is no *win-win* in stonewalling customers.

Instead, the organisation can offer options. Every officer and manager and every employee who meets, touches, or contacts a customer should be trained in scripts providing various options to resolve customer issues. Customers suspect *canned* approaches, but they are surprisingly responsive to alternative suggestions. You might offer a comparable product, reduce the price, expedite a delivery, customise packaging, and so on.

This is especially true in B2B sales, where vendors and purchasers have long-standing relationships. Your Sales Reps need authorisation and a toolkit of options to resolve problems and sustain their relationships. If the customer order received is incorrect or damaged, the organisation must respond immediately with solutions fitting the customer's expectations.

For example, replacing the incorrect order may not be the best option for the buyer, so the Sales Rep needs the authority to credit the account or replace the order's value. As an Executive Leader, you need reports tracking these errors and solutions.

- **Keep an eye on the prize.**

  CEOs and other Executive Leaders have more than enough resources for customer information. However, the volume does not guarantee power or effectiveness. No single channel has everything you need. You will need skill or advice on reading and weighing the inputs available on Facebook, Instagram, Glassdoor, and other social media.

It would be best if you were invested entirely in the product or service. It would help if you embraced it completely, so you can make the best case for its unique sales position and added values. If customer expectations are reasonable and achievable, you should address their concerns. However, when you cannot meet their expectations or their expectations are beyond satisfaction, you should eat the loss and move on. The leaders must maintain their organisation's integrity.

- **Wear values on your sleeve.**

Effective leaders must live the organisation's mission and core values. Internal and external stakeholders look to the boss for a consistent model of behaviour. You must set up a transparent system, an ecosystem where everyone has the data and tools they need to work and advance, a culture where customers trust the organisation to meet and exceed their expectations.

You might start with a qualitative analysis of the organisation's image. People expect contemporary organisations to have a mission statement, corporate vision, and core values. The website should make these themes public and prominent. Moreover, the public also expects organisation officers to take the lead on bringing those values to life.

25

You will want to ensure those values remain benchmarks for organisational behaviour. The product and services provided must align directly and clearly with those values. Consistent and authentic alignment will create and sustain trust—organisation-to-customer, organisation-to-organisation, and rank and file-to- leadership.

Legacy approaches to management have emphasised the *executive* in highly placed officers. They expect executives to drive (or *execute*) the corporate engine, make the most demanding decisions, and juggle multiple tasks in the organisation's portfolio. Today's organisation leaders must lead as much as they manage. They must embrace their role as the organisation's top sales rep, chief customer relations manager, principal market analyst, and more.

Tailoring the Customer Experience

Retail store customers represent only one experience. Still, they offer a good base on which to build a better understanding of customer experience. The *Harvard Business Review* suggests that customer experience is "*the sum-totality of how customers engage with your organisation and brand, not just in a snapshot in time, but throughout the entire arc of being a customer*" (Richardson, 2010). Moreover, those customers want a *positive* experience.

Organisations cannot wait for feedback on that experience; there is no time to be passive when you can tailor the customer experience. That is, "*companies cannot afford to throw up their hands and give up in the face of unpredictability. Instead, they need to plan for the worst and aim for the ideal when considering the experiences they want to create*" (Richardson, 2010).

- **Lead with a smile.**

  Executive Leaders must be positive and optimistic. They must offer a guiding light lifting employees' spirits to a level of good humour and constructive goodwill. If the internal customers are happy, they will share their confidence in the product and service.

  When everyone in the organisation likes what they are doing and what they are producing, they will shape the customer experience. When the organisation is tailored to stand stable and robust, the customers will pick up on that and make it part of their experience.

- **Listen creatively.**

  Despite the confidence in their organisation, Executive Leaders must listen carefully. They should understand that anything a customer says is layered with intent, perception, and opinion.

  Attentive listening "hears between the lines," so to speak. When Executive Leaders listen openly and patiently, two things will happen. First, the courtesy extended improves the experience. Second, you learn something about the product and how customers relate to it.

- **Follow the customer journey.**

Prospects and customers approach your door as a part of the journey that Executive Leaders want to understand—the more significant their customer investment, the more steps they have taken along their customer journey. You will want to put yourself in their shoes.

Customers expect some struggle in making significant investments like buying a car or home, but they still seek a smoother path. If customers are buying from your inventory—B2C or B2B, you must shorten their trip while keeping it interesting. If you remove barriers to the purchase, they need to know.

Online sales, for example, allow you to introduce gaming elements like badges, miles, and deals. However, when you structure your online presence so shoppers can compare features, visualise different colour selections, or watch videos of the product in operation, it enlivens and deepens their shopping trip engagement.

- **Help the customer own the experience.**

  Still emerging technologies help executives customise and personalise their customers' experience.

  > "*Two in five executives surveyed [by Forbes], 40%, report that their customer personalization efforts have had a direct impact on maximizing sales, basket size and profits in direct-to-consumer channels, such as e-commerce, while another 37% point to increased sales and customer lifetime value through*

product or content recommendations" (The Path to Personalization, 2020).

The *Forbes* survey also found "*46% of marketing executives are not where they want to be in terms of delivering personalization*" (The Path to Personalization, 2020).

The Internet of Things (IoT) puts immediate internet access into the hands of billions through multiple devices. The IoT expands marketing reach exponentially, but marketing is only catching up with how to use that access to customise customer experiences.

Each device has a global reach, allowing organisations to pitch them all. At the same time, each device feeds data to the organisation. It floods customer data platforms with information enabling the marketing technology to personalise its presentation. However, your organisation may not use the information it has in order to engage customers and enhance their shopping experience well.

These multiple options challenge senior executives. The possibilities present many choices, and each seems a necessity. Navigating these possibilities requires Executive Leaders to know what is available, discern what is necessary and doable, and find the assistance they need.

Customer-Centric and Agile Execution

Executive Leaders must be agile; they must have the physical and psychological ability to move and pivot when necessary. Given all their tasks and challenges, executives must be nimble enough to duck and dodge many of the things flying at them. A more optimistic view sees leaders agile enough to spot just the right position on the field or court to run the ball. Agility is also a talent for balancing, weighing and cutting to the chase.

Today's organisations must be agile enough to adapt constantly to change. Natural and catastrophic events will trigger a critical response. Political and legislative mandates may require a change. Disruptive innovation and competition will drive a significant organisational transformation.

Digital transformation is a fact of life for contemporary organisations. It continues to change every industry in ways *seen* and *unseen.* Those who have adopted modern emerging digital technologies successfully take the lead in delivering customer experiences and loyalty. Understanding an organisation's current capability, maturity, and performance is essential to building an actionable roadmap that provides incremental benefits.

However, these same organisations find they cannot drive this change when hampered by rigid hierarchical structures. They succeed better when they are *lean* and *agile.*

Executive Leaders must position their organisations to respond quickly with autonomy and great respect for collaboration. Leaders have increasingly adopted agile mindsets and methodologies where collaboration develops trust and ensures successful transformation, sustainability, and scalability.

The software development world put a new spin on *agility.* Agile thinking demands a significant behavioural transformation for the organisation. It comes at some cost and disruption, and it takes informed leadership to make it happen. "*In order to increase their ability to sense, respond and learn, organisations are up-scaling their use of agile*" (Barroca, Dingsøyr, & Mikalsen, 2019).

Agile thinking and practice bring an end to organisation "*business as usual.*" The same companies that told customers to "*like it or leave it*" now have a broad and deep customer-centric commitment and performance. Everything has been restructured to serve customers. Where profit and efficiency were once the norms, customer satisfaction has taken over. Still, the size and scope of this shift can overwhelm ill-prepared executives.

> "*The rise of Agile is driven both by the passion of those who love working this way and by organisations that are making a life-changing discovery: the only way to cope sustainably with today's marketplace is to embrace Agile*" (Denning, 2019).

Agile thinking uses a framework based on iteration, a circular rather than linear concept. Instead of letting the process flow without review, it requires mastery of team collaboration to develop solutions. The pursuit of creative and innovative responses moves standard operating procedures to the side. It disregards the "*tried and true*" and "*that's the way it's always been done*" habits.

Instead, agile thinking promotes fluid and flexible fixes for known problems and anticipated issues. Agile approaches replace legacy coercive bureaucratic hierarchies with revolutionary thinking, tools, and methodologies that enable and empower self-organizing, self-governing, and cross-functional teams. Accountability outranks responsibility, and customer experience trumps operational procedures.

Many Executive Leaders belong to a new management generation where agile disciplines inform their organisations. They understand that agile tools and methodologies require stepping up and into a new experience. Whether they have the experience or not, organisation leaders must secure outside advice and assistance to face and manage the challenges presented by transformational change and to start their agile journey to better customer experience solutions.

Here's Your Takeaway

If you are an entrepreneur, you should understand entrepreneurs often fail to identify their customers thoroughly. They tend to see themselves in the prospective customers; that is, they feel customers want and see the same things they do.

Suppose you are transitioning to another organisation or a more accountable position in your current organisation. In that case, you should analyse your prospective market well so you can bring some evidence- and data-based strategies and tactics to the table.

However your transition moves forward, Executive Leaders must immerse themselves in the customer experience's complexity to appreciate how existing and emerging technologies can achieve the organisation's goals.

The competition challenges Executive Leaders to know their customers, listen to their wants and needs, and meet or exceed their expectations. To take the lead, these leaders must master policies, processes, and practices that will enable and empower the customer satisfaction necessary to organisation growth.

Section 2

Chapter 3: The Right Trusted Advisor

Here's What to Expect

- ✓ Helping Executive Leaders
- ✓ Observing positive and negative signs
- ✓ Identifying a right Trusted Advisor
- ✓ Negotiating the agreement

For organisations embarking on any transformational change, leveraging external advice can accelerate strategy and plans and, most importantly, validate that the designed approach is sound and viable. Outside Trusted Advisors offer a wealth of expertise, such as industry or technology trends or best practices of significant added value to decision makers.

Success does not happen in a vacuum. It is not a solitary feat, but it does not have to be a lonely struggle. It should not be—when help is ready, willing, and able.

Entrepreneurs must master this lesson. Their single-minded passion and pinpoint focus run the risk of disregarding input, feedback, and governance. Their go-it-alone mindset endangers their product, service, and purpose. It stretches their capability, resilience, and health.

Organisation leaders appear to have support in numbers. They have peers and supporting managers. Still, there are tasks, strategies, and decisions that improve proportionately with the quality of their advice. Identifying, assessing, and contracting that advisor deserves the discussion that follows here.

Executive Leaders are not beyond needing advice. The scope and breadth of their accountability in volatile markets, social-economic change, and accelerating technology can challenge even the strongest executive teams. Quite often, the best executive advice is to seek top-quality advice from the outside.

Here's My Story

When working at one of the largest global banks in the world and Global 500 company leading a local merger and acquisition, it was imperative the executive leadership and board were receiving the right trusted advice.

The local operational transition was attempted twice before and failed for numerous reasons including the limited experience in executing this type of activity. This was a significant challenge with multiple external global partnerships and broader subsidiary teams that were required to come together to align on objectives and deliver to the outcomes required by the board. It was imperative for the right trusted advisor with the specialist skill sets for this outcome to be appointed and help navigate the complexities including the political landscape across organisations.

There were several critical projects in this transition that needed to deliver in the right sequence, allocated the correct prioritisation including legal and regulatory implications that could be quite catastrophic if not planned correctly. I was engaged to offer this in-depth expertise and coach the leadership on best practice transition delivery. As a result of the deep delivery experience and prudence this transition was orchestrated successfully and exceeded the board expectations.

The Need for a Trusted Advisor

COVID-19 has taught many lessons. Most organisations found themselves thrown into crisis mode without the time or resources to plan and execute properly. Disaster & Recovery Plans based on routine fire drills did not prepare them for its economic effects. It taught us that, regardless of the state of the continuity plan, today's stresses can lead you to make quick, careless decisions that have a lasting impact on an organisation's future.

Typical responses cut costs and eliminate redundancies. Ironically, this can leave the organisation too lean and ill-prepared for recovery. During crisis management, you risk leaving employees feeling undervalued. You forge ahead with some anxiety over the inadequacy of current systems to handle the changing environment.

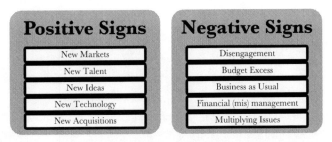

Figure 3.1: Signs You Need a Trusted Advisor

Faced with such challenges, prudent executives understand they have not secured their position because they know everything. It is not unusual to have gaps in your training, education, and experience. Still, there are positive and negative signs you may need a tight Trusted Advisor. (See Figure 3.1 and the following.)

Positive signs:

- **New Markets:**

  To identify and reach new markets, you may need help developing a strategy to rebrand and launch a new market initiative.

- **New Talent:**

  As organisations step up from start-up to growth stages, they should look for talent to transform and promise transitional future change. With some talent at a premium, your organisation may need temporary or retained advice to locate, recruit, and retain talent fit to the organisation's future.

- **New Ideas:**

  Innovation is crucial to growth. However, good ideas do not equal innovation. Securing protection for your innovation and bringing it to market requires intelligence and experience in launching innovative initiatives—experience your Executive Team may not have.

- **New Technology:**

  Advanced and emerging technologies require specially trained executive direction. Executive leaders' demands allow little room for introducing and adapting the technology futures necessary for growth and survival. You may need advice on naming what the organisation needs, where to find it, and how to bring it on board.

- **New Acquisitions:**

  Mergers and acquisitions offer exciting opportunities amidst multiple challenges. Keeping the organisation's ship afloat and even-keeled while expanding can require an experienced professional's oversight and guidance.

Negative signs:

- **Employee Disengagement:**

  Employee discontent forms an iceberg. You can see and feel the top ten percent. However, 90 percent floats below the surface.

  To fend off the iceberg or melt it down, you may need third-party input on equitable compensation and benefits, a frustrating lack of tools and resources, employee engagement and motivation, or the lack of clear direction on an organisation's goals or their respective roles in reaching them. Successful organisations thrive when employees are happy in their work; sometimes, it takes an outside advisor to see and fix the problems.

- **Budget Excess:**

  If the organisation falls short on revenue or exceeds its budget regularly, you may need someone to look at your cash flow and workflow. Something is wrong if the organisation frequently spends more than it earns. However, these problems may stem from multiple sources and need advisors strong in financial forensics.

- **Business as Usual:**

  A steady organisation may be a stale organisation. Ordinarily, stability is positive. However, stability may also signal a lack of energy, growth, and potential. It may call for someone from the outside to take a fresh look at the product, service, and lack of innovation.

- **Financial (mis) Management:**

  Financial health depends on more than spreadsheets and 12-column bookkeeping. There are compliance issues, operation flows, investment concerns, and more that only qualified consultants with a financial background can resolve. Too often, the organisation itself is not in the best position to perform adequate due diligence.

- **Multiplying Issues:**

  Lack of talent disrupted supply chains, failure to deliver, customer dissatisfaction, or legislated compliance—these issues and more can spin together to challenge Executive Leaders. The sooner they seek and retain advice, the better the organisation's potential.

You may seek help when you are tired of juggling or find too many things on your back burner. However, you should have an advisor pipeline before you find it is too late.

A Coach for That Agile Play

Agile execution is a case in point. Leaders should be able to stop, turn, and make that shot on goal whether the play has been called or not. They are expected to think on their feet and act on instinct as well as skill. However, those demands to pivot can multiply in number and intensity.

> *"A fundamental requirement of the Agile philosophy is the concept of empowered employees and a bottom-up approach to solving problems and seeking value maximization through high-performance teams. The immediate advantage of improved vertical and horizontal engagement is leveraging inherent organisational [sic] knowledge, skills, and experience"* *(Paquette & Frankl, 2016).*

Moreover, organisational potential and intellectual assets will improve. The mindset encourages informal relationships. Designers, strategists, producers, and customers forge performance connections across business units and functional silos.

Agile thinking favours aptness and adeptness, requiring the freedom and autonomy to act as needed. While you may have made that shot on goal a thousand times, sometimes you must pass to someone better positioned to make that shot in volatile game situations.

Executive Leaders are often called to make swift, graceful yet gritty, decisive moves. The ability to act with agility may be their most distinguishing characteristic. The Agile process allows:[1]

- Quick response to change based on leveraged learning,

---

[1] Based on (Hodgetts, 2004).

- Delivery of the highest business value, return on investment (ROI), and value for money (VfM),

- Decreased time-to-delivery,

- Increased productivity and efficiency,

- Better quality solutions, and

- Creation of a more fulfilling development culture.

Executive Leaders can find it tough playing offence and defence. Winning takes hyper-awareness of the entire field of play and the trust of other players in your capabilities. However, because winning also depends on your faith in others, legacy organisations must loosen up their vertical hierarchies and horizontal processes.

Agile thinking enables capabilities to multiply and strengthen. Where legacy businesses have built horizontal line processes, sequential steps feed subsequent steps in sequence, as suggested in Figure 3.2.

Figure 3.2: Legacy Horizontal Thinking

Each action consumes resources and moves results to the following stage. Subject to schedules, timelines, and accessible resources, the traditional organisation process moves forward to deliverables.

Since the past 60 years, many organisations have moved to the continuous improvement models inspired by Japanese manufacturing. Business plans are tested in action, and the lessons learned revise future execution as pictured here in Figure 3.3. It encourages immediate attention and discourages static strategies.

Figure 3.3: Continuous Improvement Model

Organisations built on the Continuous Improvement Model (CIM) and adapted it to their industry sector. Later, they would add crucial elements to this PDAC cycle. Chief among these new elements is the respect given feedback on the performance, effectiveness, or design of the brand, product, and service, as shown in Figure 3.4.

Agile projects are cyclic, iterative, and incremental. They require holistic rather than reductionist thinking. They pursue employee capabilities, target deliverables, and enhance the customer experience—not the segmented activities of horizontal processes.

Figure 3.4: Basic Agile Cycle

Finally, Agile execution emphasises team collaboration, so it works best under facilitative, enabling, and Agile executive leadership.

Agile teams often gather to form a scrum, a perfect metaphor for what happens. In rugby, an apparently carelessly arranged group of muscled forwards interlock arms and press forward against the opposing team's forwards. When the ball is thrown into this scrum, the players try to kick it toward players on their side. Figure 3.5 illustrates the Agile Cycle and Scrum.

Agile organisations promote the behaviour that interlocks talents  into a single force. While it does move forward, it does so through diverse insights, co-collaboration, shared team experiences, and creative adaptation to volatile field conditions.

Figure 3.5: Agile Cycle with Scrum

Executive Leaders must navigate transformational change and uncertainty with Agility. "*It involves clarity, connection, and confidence*" (Pruitt, 2017) and the support of a Trusted Advisor.

Identify Your Trusted Advisor

Krista Walochik, Board Chair at AESC (Association of Executive Search and Leadership Consultants), says something worth exploring:

> "*A truly Trusted Advisor is someone who puts the other party's best interest first. It requires independence, ability to form a criteria-based opinion, active listening skills and empathy, a service orientation, and the courage to challenge and say 'no' from time to time*" (The Trusted Advisor Relationship, 2020).

A Trusted Advisor puts a client's interest first. The relationship should be fiduciary; that is, Trusted Advisors must treat issues as if they were their own. They offer constructive advice as if your organisation's problems were their problems. This is crucial when dealing with financial matters, but it also applies to resources, intellectual property, customer data, human resources information, and more.

- Trusted Advisors are independent of other loyalties. Advisors tend to have a specialty so that they may provide that disciplined advice to several clients. However, they still owe your organisation their undivided attention as defined in your negotiated contract.

- Trusted Advisors need access to enough data and evidence to form reliable opinions. The quality of their advice is a direct function of accessible information.

- Trusted Advisors are quality listeners. They lean into conversations, take notes, and ask questions. They listen actively because their experience guides their inquiries, a sign of respect that executives appreciate, too.

- Trusted Advisors must establish rapport with organisation members at every level because everyone responds well to signs of respect. Empathy is the key to the feeling that the advisor is authentically present and emotionally connected with the people and their work.

- Trusted Advisors are supporters. They should not present themselves as "*equal to*" the Executive Leaders. They may partner, but their function is to serve and deliver only with executive-level consent. Nonetheless, they will need the autonomy to do their work well.

- Finally, Executive Leaders must allow the advisor to say "*no*" when necessary. A Trusted Advisor brings expert talents to the organisation, and the organisation should respect those strengths. Advisors need permission to voice a firm "no" when the evidence points that way.

Executive Leaders always have the managing role under a contract with an outside advisor. However, they should develop a trusted working partnership relationship early on. You can negotiate the contract language, but the personal connection is crucial.

Negotiating the Relationship

Executive Leaders should negotiate Trusted Advisor agreements as a "win-win" for all parties involved. Standard contracts commonly ensure scope, deliverables, and timelines, but they are not the only type of agreement available.

Trusted Advisors can protect or enhance a company's brand, sell more products or services, generate more revenue, align with a company's mission and create stronger, more loyal customers. Outcome based agreements also have a distinct advantage in that they are easy to establish and offer an opportunity for both parties to share in the risks and rewards.

However, as the organisation's Executive Leader, you must drive the contracting experience.

1. **Picture the deliverables.** Leaders have a clear picture of what deliverables they need and want. That includes calendars, costs, metrics, and outcomes.

2. **Do not surrender leverage.** The advisor has the expertise needed, but the organisation pays. Executive Leaders must not commit to charges or timetables that do not serve their needs.

3. **List realistic objectives.** The deliverables must be realistic and achievable without any surprises. Any agreement should prevent loose ends.

4. **Collaborate on an understanding** of quality and best practices. Right Trusted Advisors might arrive with recommendations, but everyone must agree on the shape, size, and test of quality inputs and outcomes.

5. **Walk away if necessary.** Negotiations conducted with mutual professionalism and respect may still not provide a level playing field on which they agree to needs, capabilities, and costs. Executive Leaders "own" their market and may be responsible for ending the negotiation and moving on.

For Example

At any growth and development stage, any organisation's Executive Leaders have primary accountability for proper governance. There are principles and practices the executives cannot always capture and monitor. Calling in a Trusted Advisor adds credibility and authority to the concerns while also allowing the leader to stay arm's length from the internal analysis.

For instance, a Trusted Advisor could examine the organisation's governance:

- **Potential conflicts of interest:**

  Conflicts of interest or the appearance of conflicts of interest have undone many highly placed executives. These are ethical and sometimes legal violations that call into question executives' behaviour and that of those reporting to them.

- **Officer liability:**

  Executive Leaders and Board Directors can stand liable for claims in litigation. They are expected to be above suspicion.

- **Transparency and accountability:**

  Well-run organisations have committed wholly to transparency and accountability that follows from full disclosure. However, they may need help in what to disclose and how to go about it.

- **Ethics:**

  Executives are expected to model excellent ethical practices throughout organisational dealings and relationships with all stakeholders. They should know—or should have known—of ethics violations.

- **Employee relations:**

  Issues of compensation, diversity, benefits, and equity can be sensitive and require third-party help.

These and other management challenges may benefit from the expertise and authority of a right Trusted Advisor. All these challenges affect organisational resilience and sustainability, strengthen the customer experience, and improve stakeholder profits.

Here's Your Takeaway

Transformation is complex and taxing. The most sophisticated and experienced Executive Leaders will tell you that you cannot manage the significant organisational or personal transition without help.

Executives who think they know it all or can do it all do not make influential leaders. Prudent executives will learn when and how to delegate initiatives, projects, and tasks. They also understand they often need a Trusted Advisor to recognise, analyse, and remedy existing or emerging issues.

It pays to name an informal personal Board of Advisors to coach you on specific needs and practices as your career progresses. They will be the first to tell you a Trusted Advisor will help relieve the decision fatigue described in the next Chapter.

Chapter 4: Decision Fatigue and What to Do About It

Here's What to Expect

- ✓ Distinguish high impact decisions
- ✓ Define "decision fatigue"
- ✓ See how decision fatigue affects management
- ✓ Seek best practices to resolve decision fatigue
- ✓ Choose a decision-making style

Executive Leaders make high-impact decisions. Making decisions takes up most of their time—as well as their physical and emotional strength.

> *"At any moment in any day, most executives are engaged in some aspect of decision making: exchanging*

information, reviewing data, coming up with ideas, evaluating alternatives, implementing directives, following up" (Brousseau, Driver, Hourihan, & Larsson, 2006).

Managing the fatigue attached to low- and high-impact decisions begins with understanding the significance of executive leaders' decisions.

The success or failure of any organisation reflects decisions made by many people at many levels. However, the decisions made at the executive level certainly can make or break an organisation's future. Executive Leaders have enhanced accountability for *doing the right thing in the right way*, and that centres on quality decision-making.

Executives are not exempt from political, economic, stakeholder, and other pressures when they make decisions. Time, people, customers, banks, governments, and other forces pressure Executive Leaders to move in one direction or another. Moreover, they are influenced by peers and subordinates. Theirs is not a simple lot.

All these pressures task their multi-tasking capacity, core character, and talent for execution. Successful executives consistently make decisions based on monitored data, collaborative input, and substantive options. They insist on the most current and relevant data; they seek and integrate diverse resources; and they have a skill for sorting and prioritising issues.

Executive Leaders do not only deal with making tough decisions within the organisation, but they also go home to struggle with family issues, personal financial problems, social obligations, and more. They must remember birthdays and anniversaries, attend children's ballet recitals and football games, and still schedule a date night or getaway weekend. Some will finance a child's college education, and some may support local political campaigns. All of them lead diverse and dynamic lives, and those lives roll out on multiple decisions.

Prudent leaders will prioritise decisions, allocate value, and balance decisions to sustain a balance among decisions related to work, family, lifestyle, and personal goals. They need a strategy to avoid decision fatigue.

Here's My Story

In working with the senior leadership team at a large Telecommunication company on a CEO sponsored transformation initiative, it became apparent they were exposed to analysis paralysis. The focus and effort of analysis was rapidly spiralling towards theoretical calculations and a series of constant "What if" questions to justify inaction. The organisation was hamstrung from executing on its strategy. The concepts of innovation, collaboration and experimentation were always raised at various leadership townhalls and meetings but when it came to applying these concepts to move forward with its strategy it stalled. It was clear that management were fatigued from the constant options being discussed over the course of this initiative. As a result, the test and learn feedback loop was a lost opportunity for as long as this constant analysis cycle perpetuated.

Within one month of working together, I had established the relationship that made them feel comfortable, and within a few weeks we were now on our way to execute the strategy with a true and accurate reflection of the landscape they were dealing with. No sugar coating, no politics, just a true independent perspective of the situation. This included a roadmap to orchestrate the outcomes they needed.

What is "Decision Fatigue?"

Everyone makes multiple decisions every day. They make choices about housework, homework, and hourly work. They make shopping, legal, and child-rearing decisions. As those choices increase in frequency and level of difficulty, they drain the brain and body's energy.

According to Roy F. Braumeister (a pioneer in this field),

> "*we use the term ego depletion to refer to a temporary reduction in the self's capacity or willingness to engage in volitional action (including controlling the environment, controlling the self, making choices, and initiating action) caused by prior exercise of volition*" (Baumeister, Bratslavsky, Muraven, & Tice, 1998).

Eventually, tired decision makers opt for shortcuts.

> "*One shortcut is to become reckless: to act impulsively instead of expending the energy to first think through the consequences...The other shortcut is the ultimate energy saver: do nothing. Instead of agonizing over decisions, avoid any choice*" (Tierney, 2011).

In simpler terms, repeated decisions affect the necessary physical, mental, and emotional capacity for prudent decision-making.

How Decision Fatigue Affects Business Decisions

Multiple sequential decisions often lead to mental exhaustion. Decisions have size (importance), speed (deadline), and weight (impact). Multiplying decisions compress these dimensions critically and disruptively, significantly when frequency increases the pressures. Repeated decisions will accelerate and negate the chance to secure and evaluate evidence and data. These "uninformed" decisions occur quickly but effectively default to the easy way out.

These quick uninformed decisions may cost the organisation money. They may ignore customer issues. Moreover, the results could offend peers, managers, employees, or shareholders.

Decision fatigue produces several unwanted outcomes:

- **Diminished judicious self-control:**

  Decision fatigue demonstrates itself in quick-to-anger and easy-to-distract moods.

- **Impulse-driven choices:**

  Impulse-driven decisions will stretch thin. Actions made on impulse are not choices at all. Impulses are irrational—hardly the result of thoughtful consideration.

- **Decision paralysis:**

  Fatigue leads to decision delay or avoidance. Like the child overwhelmed by the many options offered at an amusement park or the adult paralysed by too many choices on a menu, executives may find themselves making no choice or careless ones.

- **Trade-off confusion:**

Decision fatigue will exaggerate pressures. Executive decision makers—expected to analyse data, weigh options, seek input, and consider outcomes—may find themselves agreeing to deals without strategy or plan.

These problems often co-occur, increasing the weakness in the choices made. They are not proper decisions, so they only waste time, reduce productivity, and de-track forward progress.

Best Practice Solutions to Decision Fatigue

There are no solutions for decision fatigue unless and until you admit the problem. It can be subtle, and people often find it sneaking up on them, a sort of *fatigue creep.* There is some risk it will come to your attention only after bad decisions are behind you.

Nonetheless, Executive Leaders can and should adopt enriching habits early in their careers to forestall decision fatigue by managing decisions well and intelligently. They should assess the effects of personal habits on their anxiety and emotional balance. They should appreciate the positive impact of diet and exercise and the adverse effects of alcohol and drugs. People find it easier to maintain their balance when they have a safety net in place.

Executive Leaders will sort and arrange their decisions. They might lay out their clothes the night before, stick to the same travel arrangements, or take their meals on a schedule. Personal discipline on these minor issues frees their time for more significant issues.

You can adopt personal disciplines and improve and strengthen them with practice. Eventually, such discipline will alter your workday. Executive Leaders find ways to prioritise tasks that surround them, tasks that have no substantial role or impact on their daily work.

I suggest adopting different behaviours as models that inspire and motivate. Executive Leaders bring something to work with them, which adds value to their decision-making process and the outcomes.

The following Figure 4.1 lists some best practices in cultivating a positive decision-making mindset.

Distinguish	•essentials from non-essentials
Discern	•between low and high value
Delegate	•empower your team
Replenish	•have some fun
Win/Win	•structure mutually respectful relationships
Show Empathy	•listen well

1. **Distinguish *essential* from *non-essential* decisions.**

If you develop a healthy routine on your daily dress, commute, and breakfast and lunch items, you reduce your decision burden. You can assign other tasks like making travel arrangements, preparing for meetings, sending and receiving mail, and more. Tasks are not decisions unless you overthink them.

2. Discernment trumps decision-making.

Discernment is as much an art as a skill. It is the ability to confront a volume of material and effectively cut to its core. It pushes the unnecessary and unimportant aside to reveal value. That talent reduces the repeated confrontations presented by otherwise wrong decisions.

3. Delegate, delegate, delegate.

Delegating decisions of certain sorts at specific levels does not avoid decision-making, but it does reassign accountability. It does not pass the buck, but it forms trusting relationships with responsible and able parties. Empowering them respects their intelligence and relieves you of decision volume.

4. Shoot for Win/Win.

Executive Leaders must design win/win situations. They build a context to strengthen relationships that all stakeholders find mutually beneficial. It may not be possible to please all the people all the time, but they will buy into initiatives and decisions that serve broader organisation strategies and goals.

5. Lighten up.

Executive Leaders can relax and enjoy some personal and family time. You can set strict limits on your availability when "*off the clock.*" Even the most productive executives structure a contact chain bringing them only the most important calls. Most decisions can wait through a weekend.

6. Show empathy.

Good listeners show interest and concern for those doing the talking. Their empathy shows respect for the speaker and all who share that voice. It is the soundest base for forming strong and beneficial relationships that create a business climate where decisions come easier.

Executive Leaders pursue an agile life. They become precise at hitting targets despite the myriad physical and emotional forces swirling around them. Others around them find this steadiness and laser focus consistent and calming.

Agile thinking and methodologies favour a nimble adaptive response to the information before the decision maker. Agile executives head lean organisations where they develop strong teams able to assist, rebound, and share the small and big decisions.

Executives prone to hierarchical orders and command and control situations hold all decisions close to their vests. In doing so, they add tons to the weight of their daily work. That risks making rushed, unfounded, and poor choices. However, agile behaviour has a sort of *loose* feeling to it because it stresses a fluid dynamic.

Choice of Decision-Making Style

Organisations—looking to place or promote someone to senior executive leadership accountability—must consider a candidate's decision-making style. A record of poor decisions is discouraging. Such candidates likely decide in their personal interest, often at the expense of others. Some show behaviours symptomatic of stress and anxiety. Others repeat mistakes wasting time and money on unnecessary work and damage mitigation.

In many cases, these Executive Leaders can correct these behaviours if they recognise the problem and are willing to take corrective action. They must recognise the signals shown by the poor impression their decisions make, the tendency to vacillate to please everyone, or their refusal to accept accountability for the consequences.

The most respected Executive Leaders will admit they have made an unwise decision or two in their past. They allow and respect the constructive aspect of failure. They also can explain how they adapted their behaviour to the lessons learned.

High potential leaders will:

- simplify their lives to reduce the volume of decisions,

- assemble strong teams with the capacity to handle delegation,

- develop a sense of discernment that differentiates and prioritises decisions,

- encourage and enable a collaborative and agile approach to decision-sharing, and

- model a consistent, optimistic, and confident decision-making persona.

Prudent Executive Leaders have decided to be where they are and where they want to be. They also have decided how much of this they can do on their own and when and where they need a Trusted Advisor's input.

Workers and peers watch their Executive Leaders for decisive actions. They want to see consistent behaviours that further the organisation's purpose and growth. However, they also look for leaders to demonstrate integrity by making decisions consistent with the published vision, mission, and goals.

Here's Your Takeaway

Decision-making style remains one thing Executive Leaders control. If they suffer from decision fatigue, they must first look to themselves. Acknowledging that Executive Leaders face multilayered assaults from multiple directions, they must learn to differentiate priorities and impacts.

They must sort and delegate decisions, and they must prioritise time for their family and personal choices. Their decisions may have a high impact on their organisations, but assuming total control of decisions only weakens and undermines the organisation's sustainability.

The capability skill to delegate well may relieve fatigue, burnout, and turnover. However, it is a mark of excellence in executives transitioning and transforming themselves and their organisations.

Chapter 5: Design Your OWN Strategy

Here's What to Expect

- ✓ Recognise and respect the competition
- ✓ Apply the 5 Cs in "me-too" approaches
- ✓ Learn how to own your OWN strategy
- ✓ Form a unique value proposition

We all seek a "new normal" in these disruptive days. We feel disruption at all levels. The range of options open to Executive Leaders seeking to transform their organisations can be overwhelming. The opportunities present a multidimensional dilemma for even the strongest Executive Leaders.

It is often appealing to chase the latest and greatest innovations; however, organisations vary dramatically and often approach change from an entrenched culture at different maturity levels.

Besides, vendors provide endless ideas and solutions for current and emerging problems. However, the success of competitor models is most often not suitable for your organisation's needs.

Designing the right transformational strategy must begin with leaders who have a vision for the future. What type of company do they want to be? What level of Customer Service do they want to provide? How do they want to deliver their products and services? You must establish these core pillars early and let them drive you to develop the buy-in to succeed.

Executive Leaders must brand their experience. They make a real difference and leave a lasting impression. They provide a unique experience, create history, and deserve credit for the work. However, the best of them is not ego-driven.

Of course, they are self-confident and proud of their achievements. They are often magnetic and charismatic personalities. Still, strong leaders align well with their organisation's purpose, product, and people.

Successful organisations have Executive Leaders capable of developing and implementing strategies producing deliverables unique to the market and customer experience. For an organisation to establish and sustain its position, it requires leaders who own their accountability.

"Owning" has little to do with material possession but everything to do with self-possession. These people are comfortable aligning their performance with that of the organisation and modelling how their product or service makes a striking difference.

Owning a strategy and knowing how to structure, communicate, and execute the strategy takes insight, passion, and courage in the face of today's threats.

Here's My Story

A client with global reach competed by cloning the competitor's product offering. This 'me-too' approach resulted in catastrophic financial losses for several reasons.

Once engaged to recommend options to the CEO, I found the root cause was an extremely risk-averse corporate culture and governance models that prevented innovation. Their corporate structure was not set up to trust nor delegate authority to senior staff members to test and learn.

Instead, their bureaucratic structures meant that a 'replicate/me-too' model would ensure positive feedback from the financial oversight committee members. However, this approach lacked independent review from the various capability teams, including the customer experience team, who would provide the right level of insight from internal operations and external customer perspectives.

THE LEADERSHIP SHIFT

Together with the executive team we focused the implementation of the product roadmap on innovation with appropriate risk measures - leveraging the internal capabilities and skillsets of the organisation. This collaboration created a cross-functional group of Senior Directors and Vice Presidents to collaborate on organisational vision, outcomes, products, and operational strategies, including a transformational digital paradigm. This new leadership team built its own strategy focused on customer experience rather than the competitor's work.

What the Competition Has to Say

Healthy organisations build upon robust strategies authored by solid executives. However, there is more to it than that. Their strategies are unique to the organisation. That is, executives must stay focused on their unique sales proposition. They must drive their design towards an agreed-upon end. They should optimise their talents to that end, seek assistance and support where needed, and achieve deliverables consistent with their unique sales promise.

Moreover, they must do this despite the competition. There is always a strong temptation to watch the competition. Indeed, it would be naïve to ignore the competitors' strengths. There is essential information in the competition's performance. They may be strong in specific markets, deliver innovative solutions, or provide something different in customer experience.

You can access competitor information on several platforms:

- **Media**

  Competitors exploit multiple platforms, from signage to print advertising to digital messaging to social media and more. It is important to know what they do to reach their current and future markets. Their content and how others interact with their efforts may reveal openings for your intrusion and disruption.

- **Feedback**

  Dissatisfied customers create a new market worth serving. Competitors become a market focal point for feedback.

Sales prospects and customers are quick to comment on brand performance. The competitor may have a fine product, but if the market complains about the size, variety, applicability, delivery, and other features, that could offer an opportunity to enter or capture that market.

- **Motivation**

  Competition makes everyone work harder to please and hold their respective market segments. Success by one organisation prompts others to step up. When an Organisation "X" tweaks its leading product or service, Organisations "Y" and "Z" will follow. Moreover, if price differentiation follows, the entire customer base benefits.

- **Data**

  Competitors' data can teach how to do things right. Success is tangible. It has metrics that identify and define it. These can help executives to develop their strategic approach to specific market segments, demographics, and regions. Data on their success can influence product design and functionality. Finally, success in competition depends on your ability to read between the competitor's unique sales proposition lines.

However, all too often, organisations decide to imitate what they see happening. Then, one organisation rushes to the market with an almost indistinguishable approach from someone already there. Me-too strategies have indeed worked. "Me-too" organisations compete every day in everything from fast food burgers to smartphones. Organisations do make money with a focus on being in second or third place.

However, respecting what the competition does well should not encourage imitation. A me-too strategy that seeks to replicate the competition's approach is limited in vision and unproductive in the long run.

Problems with Me-Too Approaches

The competition does require your attention. However, slavish attention takes away from more important work. Obsession with following the competition takes focus away from the unique properties, features, and benefits you are branding as your own. Even where your organisation targets the same market as the competition, you will serve that market better with a strategy of your own making; a strategy you OWN.

Stakeholders will hold executives responsible for the outcomes of their strategies despite the many factors involved. It makes sense for leaders to design, communicate, and implement their strategy, so it differs from the competition. It should be original in concept and delivery.

There are at least five reasons to make your strategy stand alone. You might remember them as *"The 5 Cs"*:

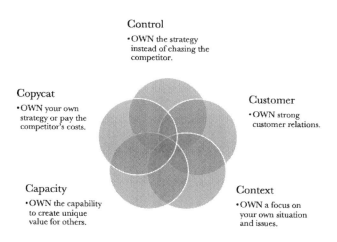

Control
•OWN the strategy instead of chasing the competitor.

Copycat
•OWN your own strategy or pay the competitor's costs.

Customer
•OWN strong customer relations.

Capacity
•OWN the capability to create unique value for others.

Context
•OWN a focus on your own situation and issues.

Figure 5.1: The 5 CS to Make Your Strategy Stand Alone

1. Control

You have no control over the competition, so pursuing a "me-too" strategy offers them some advantage. A "me-too" organisation always chases from behind only to find itself swept up or thrown aside by the stronger competitor.

2. Customer experience

Focus on a strong customer experience will secure and sustain customer loyalty. It forms an emotional connection to a brand that looks beyond competition for benefits of interest to them. Customers and consumers believe they have a problem, and it is your job to offer a satisfying solution. Happy customers will not look at the competition.

3. Context

The competition has its own history. It fights its own battles, meets its own challenges, and answers to its own stakeholders. If they do well, they must manage these issues well. There is no value in imitating their product or service because they have come from that different context. You must understand your context and focus on satisfying its interests.

4. Capacity

Imitation consumes your organisation's resources. This is costly for new organisations. A me-too habit wastes time, energy, material, and capital resources following someone else's target. The same effort pays off when focused on creating your OWN unique sales proposition by creating and delivering a product or service attractively different from the competition.

5. Copycat

Organisations reduce innovation when they copy each other. If a business squanders its capital and energy replicating the competition, the only result is a slight spin on the existing. When Organisation "B" tweaks Organisation "A"'s product line, Organisation "B" loses motivation to do something new and unique.

Each of these problems comes at a cost. Imitation impacts budgets, brand reputation, learning rates, and employee morale. Losses and risks increase because chasing the competition underestimates customer perception and experience. Imitation, in other words, incurs the competitor's negative issues.

How to OWN Your Strategy

Executive Leaders must take ownership of their organisation's strategy from the start. It takes research into marketing analysis, design, and execution.

> *"A strategy is a long-term plan that you create for your organisation to reach the desired, future state you envision. A strategy includes your organisation's goals and objectives, the type of products/services that you plan to build, the customers who you want to sell to and the markets that you serve to make profits"* (Reddy, 2018).

The most successful organisations follow this lead. However, this assumes their Executive Leaders have strengths in several factors that integrate with a strong strategy. They must have a fully shared vision, a determined commitment to its fulfilment, and an understanding that collaboration is key to achievement. The strategy will falter if any of these talents are absent.

Having designed a strategy and framed the journey to achieve the goals, Executive Leaders must use concrete language. They should illustrate the Objectives and Key Results using gauges, thermometers, or scales. They should also display dashboards where teams and other employees can watch the progress.

Some employers have put such dashboards on their websites. They have made the dashboard a home page for all employee computers. Finally, they encourage feedback from every participant or observer.

Executive Leaders must focus on key performance metrics:

☑	**Articulate**	*Communicate a clear strategy*
☑	**Visualise**	*Draw vivid pictures*
☑	**Leverage**	*Respect diverse talents*
☑	**Price**	*Offer value for money*
☑	**Market**	*Pursue new opportunities*

Figure 5.2: 5 Metrics for Owning Your OWN Strategy

1. Articulate

A strategy must be clear, articulated in an easy-to-remember phrase. There is good psychology in reducing everything you have in mind to one simple sentence.

A robust and well-phrased statement makes sense to peers, management, employees, and customers. A memorably phrased strategic purpose aligns all stakeholder interests with the same path. It is the constant against which everyone will measure effort and achievement.

2. Visualise

Successful executives have a talent for seeing things differently. They do not just see a product. They envision their product in use. In their eyes, it changes and enriches their customers' experience. They design strategies that produce multi-dimensional experiences. They are not horizontal thinkers; instead, their talent makes holistic experiences familiar. Their strategies, then, pursue dynamic and fluid lines.

3. Leverage

Ironically, to OWN your strategy, you must leverage the talents of your colleagues and advisors. In a collaborative mode, you respect all stakeholders' inputs in mapping a path reflecting their reality and capacity.

Entrepreneurs sometimes resist moving forward with others. Many of them push forward without help because they are passionate about their plans.

However, the most successful people understand the value of shared work and purpose. They will recruit talent and seek counsel on the skills they need. Every leader should have a personal Board of Directors supporting issues ranging from venture capital to human capital.

4. Price

With a strong focus on product design, development, and delivery, any organisation can become a premier provider. As a premium provider, you can supply the demand at higher prices. The higher prices, then, allow the organisation to earn more while working less.

Price has little connection with the cost incurred in the production. Instead, the customer decides the price by buying or not buying. To maintain a preferred revenue flow, organisation leadership must invest in branding, presentation, and customer experience that build customers' Value for Money.

5. **Market**

While committed to customer satisfaction, you risk becoming locked into a static context. However, "*Noncustomers, not customers, hold the greatest insight into the points of pain and intimidation that limit the boundary of an industry*" (Kim & Mauborgne, 2015).

Keeping attention on current customers may press organisations to meet or beat the competition. However, it also keeps them from recognising or exploring *blue ocean* opportunities, new markets where your unique strengths can capitalise.

Forming a Promising Value Proposition

A value proposition makes a promise to customers. It tells them what the organisation stands for, and it pictures the unique reason they should buy. The proposition summarises the organisation's intent and why that is important to the customer.

The value proposition or unique sales proposition offers a pitch to potential customers that your product or service does more for them than the competition. The emphasis is on the specific virtue or value added to their shopping experience.

Where investors look for a Return on Investment (ROI), customers seek Value for Money (VfM) ROI is easily calculated as a percentage of financial gain (or loss) on the financial investment. VfM is a more subtle customer perception of the utility of the purchase.

Customers determine the lowest purchase price (economy), but they also value the product or service's efficiency and effectiveness. Your organisation's value proposition must target these "3 Es": *economy, efficiency,* and *effectiveness.* Executives must appreciate that their target's perception of value applies to meaningful use and application. In other words, customers must feel some added weight—above and beyond the attractive asked-for price.

Successful organisations communicate their value proposition regularly and directly through branding on websites, social media, collateral marketing materials, and other advertising. You might consider the value incentive offered by the following significant organisations in their own words:

- **Amazon** — "Amazon is guided by four principles: customer obsession rather than competitor focus, passion for invention, commitment to operational excellence, and long-term thinking."

- **Goodman Group** — "Goodman is a global property group. We own, develop and manage industrial real estate in 17 countries including logistics and industrial facilities, warehouses and organisation parks."

- **Under Armour** — "Under Armour's vision is to inspire you with performance solutions you never knew you needed and can't imagine living without."

- **Wesfarmers** — "Delivering value today and tomorrow."

- **Woolworth's Group** — "We are on a mission to deliver the best in convenience, value, and quality for our customers."

A clear value proposition helps an organisation build and sustain strategic success because it justifies pricing, differentiates one approach from another, and inspires customer loyalty.

Employees and customers are quick to tell you if the deliverables do not align with the promise, so owning the strategy from the start increases in importance.

- **Pricing**

A me-too strategy will launch its new product by undercutting the competitor's price. This may have short-term success. However, if the customer finds the quality lacking, there is no real gain. It makes more sense to price a product correctly for the value added by your organisation's unique differentiation. Loyal buyers are discerning shoppers; in the long run, they will opt for Value for Money.

- **Engagement**

An organisation needs an engaging message, one that sets the product apart. Engaged by brand symbol, name, and reputation, shoppers will reach for the exceptional item at a price they can afford. Established excellence makes their decisions easier.

- **Loyalty**

Price makes a difference, but customers only return when they found value at that price. High-performing organisations seek to develop customer loyalty, focusing on textured customer experience, one that offers additional rewards and sustainable relationships.

- **Scalable**

  Building a loyal customer base provides new leverage. With reliable revenues, you gain economies of scale that enable and empower product improvement and innovation supported by customer feedback as much as research and development.

The competition has an important role. However, influential Executive Leaders design and deliver their OWN strategy. Knowing what they do and how they justify their claims provides essential data for your decision-making. However, this can lead to *a me-too strategy* that proves costly and produces limited results.

Pursuing your OWN strategy does not mean pursuing personal self-interest. Instead, an effective marketing strategy must reflect contributions from all functional leaders. The strategy must reflect the collaboration of finance, R&D, operations, logistics, and more. Your OWN strategy depends on buy-in from the bottom up. The stronger that commitment, the more success you will find.

OWNing the strategy has nothing to do with possession. It refers to the design and launch of a unique framework. Marketing leads may have something to say about the competition. The competitors have shown some values, or they would not pose a threat. Taking OWNership means tweaking and adapting some things that work in the marketplace. However, the OWNership comes with adding value in process, tools, quality, and customer experience.

Here's Your Takeaway

Many an organisation sets out to imitate its competition. After all, the competitors have done the legwork and made the initial investment. Such organisations think it just makes sense to ride the competition's coattails.

However, there is no tangible benefit to "me-too" strategies. Hugely successful competition and growth come from unique products and positions.

Executive Leaders will benefit from advances made by organisations with similar products, services, markets, and purposes. However, they must define something unique about their proposition and how they will achieve the success they seek.

Successful Executive Leaders set themselves and their organisations apart by identifying the Value for Money their prospective customers expect.

If you are to build a deliverable strategy, you need a roadmap. Participants and customers must know where they are going and recognise the achievable milestones as they pass.

Chapter 6 should help you understand why the roadmap needs your holistic and dynamic approach.

Chapter 6: Building the Incremental Benefit Roadmap

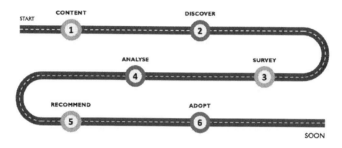

Here's What to Expect

✓ The need for a strategic roadmap
✓ Understanding the emerging approach
✓ Drawing clear pictures
✓ Creating a strategy of alignment
✓ Finding an agile solution

Today's organisations cannot afford long lead times or "Big Bang" approaches to realise benefits. In the current business environment, it is far more effective to realise benefits incrementally. Doing so provides a rapid mechanism to test and learn the effectiveness of a new product or service while refining and tuning based on customer feedback. Excessively long lead times in releasing products and services to market risks missing opportunities and critical market feedback early enough in the process.

Legacy approaches to organisation management followed strict vertical hierarchies. Power and authority were distributed from the top, and positions in the tiers below were defined by the range and scope of their authority. People at the bottom level had little or no power over their work.

Legacy approaches to project management owed a great deal to the horizontal delivery of procurement systems. This horizontal thinking reduced processes to units, each of which succeeded the previous and carried forward its content. The result of the chain was an aggregate of the preceding steps.

Neither the vertical or horizontal approaches of these organisations allowed for the dynamic at the core of most creative and responsive processes required today. They do not permit the flexibility, fluidity, or freedom that ensures quality and high-impact outcomes in a world of global access, immediacy, and demand.

In these traditional approaches, adherence to orders, policies, and procedures discouraged feedback, input, and innovation. They disabled corrective action and positive deviance. Their systems were based on restraint rather than value, adaption, and scalability.

Executive Leaders do better when they adopt agile strategies requiring co-creation, collaboration, and consensus. They should make decisions and create enabling work environments built on alignment rather than vertical or horizontal infrastructures.

In these contemporary environments, the short- and long-term plans are illustrated on a Strategy Roadmap. Executive Leaders must direct, monitor, and participate in developing this roadmap. The process aligns their respective functional interests, talents, and accountabilities—integrating them into a common purpose. However, they may need help preparing and executing an effective Strategy Roadmap.

Here's My Story

During a recent engagement on a large transformation that encompassed multiple global enterprise organisations, significant challenges surfaced around employee engagement and loss of corporate knowledge. The importance of undertaking due diligence cannot be underestimated. The discovery process uncovered several problem areas that hindered the organisation's ability to launch new capabilities. There was one clear root cause, namely a 'big bang' approach to program delivery. Leadership had failed to understand the benefits of the incremental delivery process.

The broader organisation teams also struggled to understand the agile approach and were unclear of the implications of an incremental delivery process. For example, the capital funding process hindered the team from being able to fund the agile team for a 'test and learn' and ultimately deliver incremental benefits. As a result, the organisation stumbled through 'analysis paralysis', continuing to avoid program commitment because of the lack of benefit realisation in the short term.

I was tasked to orchestrate a governance model and help define an incremental delivery roadmap that would deliver tangible benefits in short timeframes and build confidence in the strategy. The key to success was providing a trusted and independent perspective that ensured a fit for purpose model that would provide the outcomes the organisation was seeking.

The Emerging Approach

Projects, programs, and portfolios are complete as soon as they deliver their objectives. Managers then move on to the following order. This has often been imagined as a straight-through process where the project consumes resources incrementally as it rolls out.

However, the mental picture of "success" has changed. According to the Project Management Institute (PMI),

> "*Success has numerous definitions, but one way to think about it is to view it as contingent on making predictions and meeting commitments relative to products, services, or results and* **providing sustainable benefits for customers and end-users in the process**" (Linger, 2015).

In time, strategic thinkers have seen the value in visualising the fluid dynamic of organisation planning. They have pictured continuing progress as cyclic and integrative.

The executive focus should be on providing **benefits**. While the individual executives may have designated functional responsibilities, their overall accountability lies in aligning their strategies and tactics to provide sustainable customer benefits, a dramatic shift from the traditional concentration on profit and loss.

Much of the 20th-century treated producers as machines. They had to be well-oiled and cost-effective. Budgets ruled productivity, and shareholders determined policy. However, today's organisations are lean and customer-focused, requiring a paradigm shift in culture, performance, and executive leadership.

As Executive Leaders embrace agile methodologies, they appreciate the rapid iteration and testing for the continuous learning and improvement they enable. They trust invention and innovation in empowered teams' hands accountable for rapid reflection, reconsideration, and reconfiguring solutions.

Today's Executive Leaders have come to value the agile focus on rapid iteration and experimentation. That is, agile teams deliver benefits very quickly in *sprints*. Without losing their anchor in shared vision and purpose, teams report progress, solve problems, and realign direction frequently.

Team members still meet to review and replan. They share their respective progress to date, and they set goals for the next strategic steps. In legacy hierarchies, the organisation's machinery depended on the engineering and alignment of its gears. In agile traditions, each turn of the agile cycle learns something new to carry forward. Each turn or iteration drives experimentation, which then produces new understanding and information.

 Agile thinking and methodologies empower quick solutions to arising challenges. This reduces rework, waste, and time. There is nothing linear, horizontal, or "straight" about agile approaches, as Figure 6.1 shows.

Figure 6.1: Illustrates a single iteration

They rely on a chain in which work cycles through development, deployment, and discernment phases. Products or services are created and tested in-house—and in the marketplace.

Now, imagine a sequence of these reiterations. Figure 6.2 illustrates these cycles as a helix. The image suggests the dynamic continuity of a self-improving process.

Figure 6.2: Agile Helix

This iterative cycling uses the resulting data to discern what improvements are necessary and achievable. Each iteration of the process, thus, contributes to continuous improvement.

Agile thinking focuses less on forecasting and trending. Instead, it approaches work as the sum of incremental benefits. While some executives may focus on the incremental costs of labour, materials, energy, and so on, agile thinkers emphasise the benefits of taking one direction or another when decisive challenges present themselves.

Draw Big – and Little – Pictures

Executive Leaders must foster the ability to visualise their strategy. The ability to draw big and little pictures helps share and integrate their understanding. A Strategy Roadmap does that well; it helps others see, understand, share, and buy into an illustration of the organisation's direction.

Customers buy benefits. The features of a product or service produce the benefits. However, given that different stakeholders value different benefits, any process includes multiple participants accountable for the implementation of the benefits. To manage, measure, and monitor the process, they need an Incremental Benefits Roadmap.

A roadmap differs from a plan. Where a plan covers the *how,* a Strategy Roadmap defines the *what, when,* and *why.* While a plan shows the execution, the Strategy Roadmap identifies the purpose and drivers. A plan follows straight lines with attention to numbers, percentages, dollars, dates, and metrics.

However, a Strategy Roadmap offers leaders, managers, and frontline support a picture of the changes, adaptations, and adjustments that must remain aligned with the organisation's strategic vision. It provides a theme of resilience, readiness, and urgency.

Executive Leaders have multiple obligations in front of them. Front line managers are tasked with single projects with specific end dates and metrics. However, executives—individually and as a group—manage several assignments that may involve conflicts in resource allocation, the overlap in time and talent consumption, and the integration of complex systems. A Strategy Roadmap puts all this on the wall.

Typically, a Strategy Roadmap might include the following:

- A **clear statement** of the organisation's priorities,
- Illustration of the **timeline** for project achievement,
- Indication of **alignment** linking project and organisation goals to satisfy customer experience,
- **Estimated costs** of each project, and
- The **accountable executive**'s name for each project.

Any strategic roadmap should model a shared purpose and vision through alignment and prioritisation. It also should incorporate stakeholder feedback and set clear outcomes expected at all levels.

Project Management tends to rely heavily on versions of spreadsheets and Gantt charts or other horizontal dashboards.

For them, a Strategy Roadmap might look something like the following Figure 6.3.

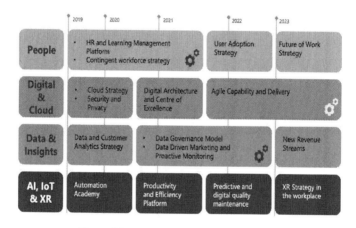

Figure 6.3: Five-Year Technology Roadmap

Incremental benefit roadmaps may resemble project management plans. However, project management focuses on scheduling tasks in time and within budget whereas an incremental benefit roadmap stresses alignment, accountability, and benefit-producing actions. It is a methodology of applying incremental changes so that the organisation can measure and judge the success of their changes. Furthermore, it will allow a more accurate assessment of what effect each new change has, while also giving the opportunity for adjustments if needed before proceeding with additional steps against the overall strategy and outcomes.

Realising the strategy requires the company to be clear about what is important what is not. Alignment and empowerment are crucial ingredients to a successful roadmap that will be the foundation for executing against the organisational strategy. Aligning the team to the strategy requires a clear vision and a shared purpose while empowering the teams to take ownership of the outcomes.

While the internet offers many templates for Incremental Benefit Roadmaps, you will find them bare-boned at best. They may provide guidelines, but you must customise yours to the organisation in the context of its current and foreseen environments.

For instance, product manufacturers may align their roadmaps with quantitative metrics, but their plans must also respect qualitative and customer satisfaction measures. These will differ from one manufacturer to another. Likewise, organisations that provide services must identify the Key Performance Indicators that define their growth.

These variations will shape various Incremental Benefits Roadmaps specific to the organisation's mission and purpose.

Mapping a Strategy of Alignment

An effective Strategy Roadmap illustrates the journey the organisation has in mind. Success rarely follows a straight line. There will be hurdles and barriers, some expected and some not.

The journey always has multiple participants, each of which follows a functional path; for example, finance, operations, research and development, marketing, and more will follow their respective disciplines. However, all these paths must integrate to align with shared interests and purpose. Executives must define, assert, and communicate these values (the *why*) and determine the methods, tactics, and resources necessary to achieve the desired ends (the *what* and *when*).

Mapping these aspirations over 10 to 15 years takes more than straight routes. The pathways will merge and diverge naturally; they will intersect at times and run parallel at others. However, Executive Leaders take paths aligned with stakeholder investment in the unique sales proposition and ultimate customer experience.

There is no standard or best organisation vision:

> "*organisations have been equally successful with visions focused on improving cost, growth, market share, sales, or even external constraints. What matters is that the organisation finds the right vision for itself and then communicates and pursues it in a way that is concrete, relevant, and meaningful to individuals*" (Mautin, 2014).

The Strategy Roadmap should show where functional paths integrate, blending their power, energy, and performance to achieve the articulated vision.

- **Align individuals and teams with organisational purpose.**

Each organisational role must align to achieve short- and long-term goals. The participant roles include invested stakeholders as well as present and future customers. Mapping alignment for these roles requires a top-down understanding of the nature and purpose of individual organisation jobs and functions.

The individuals holding those positions participate in teams formed and fitted to launch and complete projects. Teams will not coalesce in thought or action if the members do not know how to embrace the organisation's vision.

That vision provides the context in which they function. Then, Executive Leaders must define the teams' relationship to the organisation's larger purpose and model the behaviour necessary to sustain that vision.

- **Connect employees to organisational goals.**

In the past, organisations emphasised how resources and processes flow through to the customer. They positioned themselves as part of a supply chain. However, new approaches put the customer experience at the centre of each organisation's people and their respective functions.

Leaders are finding more success in threading a sense of emotional connectedness throughout the operation. They have confidence in their people and the talents they bring to the table. They trust them to buy into analysis and solutions in committed collaboration with diverse peers.

Executive Leaders foster an environment and culture built on mutual and reciprocal respect. They regularly and authentically acknowledge the work, innovation, and achievements of organisation members. This sense of connectedness surrounds common goals with an increased commitment to success. Everyone thus becomes an invested stakeholder.

- **Remove barriers and potholes.**

  Executive Leaders are expected to remove the barriers and fill the potholes on the road to success. Everyone looks to them to get things out of the way on the Strategy Roadmap.

  Executive Leaders will drive efforts to reach the organisation's goals. However, they have a more significant task in keeping everyone focused. They must not only supply the necessary resources and tools, but they must also provide the training and support to optimise performance. People (including customers) look to Executive Leaders for guidance, energy, and passion. They want leaders to model the behaviour necessary to navigate the Strategy Roadmap.

- **Maximise communication on alignment.**

  Organisation goals should be phrased simply. They should contain keywords or phrases, and all organisation communications should repeat those terms. That essential vocabulary should appear in team language, signage around the facility, newsletters, press releases, agendas, speeches, and other communication to the membership.

"*Today's collaboratively-minded employee expects communication to be a two-way street*" (Beheshti, 2019). One study shows, "*Employees who feel their voice is heard are 4.6 times more likely to feel empowered to perform their best work*" (Beheshti, 2019).

Constant and consistent communication keeps everyone aligned with common interests. Another study by *Officevibe* reports,

> "*four out of 10 workers are actively disengaged when they get little or no feedback; 82% of employees appreciate positive and negative feedback; and 43% of highly engaged employees receive feedback at least once a week as opposed to 18% of low engagement employees*" (Lyons, 2017).

Executives must enable feedback, assess its value, integrate helpful input, and recognise the contributors. Individuals are looking for acknowledgment, respect, and acceptance that they have taken paths supporting the Strategy Roadmap. An open and enabling dialogue will engage and focus everyone's efforts.

An Agile Solution

Agile thinking, methodologies, and tools assume much of the preceding content. Agile thinking avoids horizontal approaches as rational and reductionist. It prefers to approach things in circles; that is, it assumes a limber, improvisational, and ad hoc capability to anticipate and address problems with the fast and deft response to expected and unexpected issues.

Agile environments encourage periods of cross-functional meetings called Scrums. The Scrum gathers like football players to bring the most appropriate talents and voices to new negative variances from the plan. Their assigned dynamic recognises and assesses arising problems and collaborates on innovative resolutions. It is their job to set things up for the best shot at the goal.

However, this focus risks taking attention away from *The Big Picture.* So, even the electric and engaging Agile orientation needs a roadmap to keep its inputs and outputs aligned with organisation goals.

- A clear vision articulates the organisation's purpose. The roadmap shows how individual and integrated contributors fuel that purpose.

- The Strategy Roadmap requires milestones, well-understood metrics that assess people's progress, processes, and products. In an Agile climate, the roadmap should help ensure consistency across functional silos, product and service lines, and distant locations.

- Scrums work on *themes* or aspects of the program or project. Executive Leaders select members for their experience with individual themes. However, the roadmap directs their short-term independence to larger long-term goals.

- A Strategy Roadmap needs continuity and forward motion. Roadmap designers have the challenge of creating a fluid and flexible plan that also has scalability and sustainability. Drawing the roadmap helps clarify and minimise priorities. Designers must build in adaptive currency without changing the direction too often.

- A good roadmap will anticipate the development and introduction of new products and services. With its focus on organisation goals, the map will keep those developments aligned.

Designing, creating, and executing a strategic roadmap is a challenge. It takes a clear understanding of the organisation's purpose because it integrates multiple paths to deliver incremental benefits at defined milestones. It takes mental agility to align all these functions, and it takes talent to express the strategy in a visible roadmap. Most organisation leaders will seek outside advice on the roadmap's preparation and execution.

Here's Your Takeaway

Advanced and accelerating technology will design and run organisation administration and operations well into the future, thoroughly changing the worker and customer experience.

Because some of that acceleration will be under your control and some will not, your best strategy now is to draw an incremental benefit roadmap, one that reflects where your organisation is on a past, present, and future timeline.

That roadmap must illustrate the Pain Points, Touchpoints, and Pivot Points to ensure future aspiration. That means:

- ✓ drawing a vivid storyboard that shares the vision,
- ✓ showing the paths that align functions, processes, and people with enhanced customer experience,
- ✓ recognizing the benefits of Agile infrastructure and performance, and
- ✓ optimising operations.

Chapter 7: Leveraging Technology Advancements and Innovation

Here's What to Expect

- ✓ Understanding technology
- ✓ 10 Technology challenges
- ✓ Innovation and Invention
- ✓ Leveraging technology in the organisation
- ✓ Best practices to optimise technology

Accelerating Technology innovation provides game-changing opportunities across the entire business sector and helps drive enormous efficiency gains and exceptional customer service. No matter the objective of any transformation, technology will play a key enablement role.

While organisations continue to leverage proven technologies (e.g., Customer Management Systems), how businesses should approach still emerging technology holds significant promise.

Successful approaches include "proofs of concepts"—partnering with the solution provider to deploy, test, and roll out the proposed technology to a small userbase for feedback. When "proved" successful, they can scale the technology to more users.

However, should the technology prove "not fit for purpose," the impacts (both in terms of investment and expectations) are much easier to manage. Notably, the process will leverage key learning and understanding going forward.

"Leveraging" refers to the strategic use of a tool to lift or move some barrier to achievement. A shovel is a technology used to ease labour. However, the "technology" examined here refers to the tools defining the Information Age and Digital Generation. Used well, it can move mountains; however, this requires understanding and strategy to overcome challenges. Done right, this leveraging can affect organisational transformation.

Technology began to dominate organisations as hardware and software designed to speed, sort, and archive records. It had a significant impact on Accounting, for example. Other skills and functions soon saw value in technology's potential. It leveraged Human Resources records, Purchasing habits, and Operations and Inventory.

Providers and end users began to innovate with the emerging tools and applications to accelerate sales, reach globally, increase quality, reduce costs, and significantly improve the customer experience. These goals challenge Executive Leaders to understand their needs, seek the best-trusted advice, and ensure their organisation's success.

Here's My Story

During a recent engagement in a large multi-national organisation, a difficult decision surrounding a significant technology investment required in depth analysis and executive leadership alignment. With differences in opinion amongst the leadership team, including options on building internal capability or leveraging a partnership technology / Commercially off-the-shelf (COTS) capability, it was increasingly difficult to drive a decision and a path forward. There were many advantages and disadvantages for the different options.

An extensive due diligence exercise was commissioned to, amongst other things, define the key design principles and ultimately align the leadership team. The key principles included (i) flexibility for third party integrations; (ii) owning end-to-end customer experience; and (iii) building the foundation for future technology advancements. As a result, it was determined that the technology would be developed internally to ensure the best possible customer experience is provided and to enable the organisation for continuous improvements.

THE LEADERSHIP SHIFT

One of the key successes in this case was that I was able to create a governance structure that respects the diversity of talent and insights. Such a consideration is critical when undertaking significant and transformative decisions.

Understanding Technology

"Technology" is often a misused term. An overarching definition holds that "technology" is *"the application of scientific knowledge to the practical aims of human life or, as it is sometimes phrased, to the change and manipulation of the human environment" (Augustyn, 2018).* Practically speaking, you do not find it used in this sense often.

Technology evokes images of things—computers, iPhones, banking ATMs, drones, and more. These innovations repeatedly appear in daily life. Some have a more immediate and personal impact than others. Others operate below the surface, making life more comfortable without being noticed. Some change the world in big ways like faster airline flights, lifesaving medications, or deadly weapons of war.

Technology is the study of technique, *a science of how things get done.* That covers so many things like how they sew clothes, milk cows, send messages, process sales orders, make deliveries, and more. Scientists, engineers, architects, and others research and develop inventions and innovations to make things easier, efficient, and effective for people.

"Technology" commonly refers to the development and deployment of innovations in communication. Most people only focus on the competitive changes in smartphones, with manufacturers reporting advances in their phones' capabilities each year. However, that narrow focus ignores advances in medical devices, self-driving vehicles, manufacturing automation, and elsewhere.

So, *technology* labels *the broad aggregation of tools, experience, discipline, and products that directly and indirectly change the human experience.*

Any approach to understanding and leveraging technology at your organisation involves:

1. **Accumulating**, mining, and evaluating newly accessible and expanding data,

2. **Managing** the technology that supports marketing analysis, strategic alignment with customer experience, and sustainable and scalable decisions,

3. **Differentiating** invention from innovation,

4. **Avoiding** technology with a negative impact on the social and environmental ecosystems, and

5. **Optimising** employee and customer experience.

This all challenges you to step up your game, learning how to apply and operate the new ways of doing things. The lack of understanding technology in broad and narrow senses leads to challenges paralleling the needs just listed:

1. Technology produces high-volume and high-speed data that organisations too often ignore or fail to utilise effectively.

2. Most executives lack the talent or insight to maximise the technology supporting decision-making.

3. Organisation leaders confuse invention and innovation, thereby missing high-impact results.

4. Intentionally or not, they introduce technology indifferent to, disruptive of, or dangerous to ecosystems, and

5. They may use technology that disrupts and endangers employee and customer experience.

This chapter hopes to tackle this complex issue. It seeks to clarify the technology challenges facing Executive Leaders and suggest ways to economically, efficiently, and effectively leverage its potential.

In complex and global organisations, local factors can complicate the technology needed and used. Moreover, the pace at which these functions advance can be overwhelming.

Still, Executive Leaders must interact with these specialised talents and services. They may not stay on top of everything in the technology universe. Still, they must know enough of the jargon and functionalities to make sound strategic choices on technology purchases and implementation.

10 Technology Challenges

Given what the technology umbrella covers, executives find themselves facing at least ten challenges:

1. Cybersecurity

In-house, local, regional, and international interests may have authorised access to vital proprietary information. However, the organisation must protect the personnel information, trade secrets, patents, financials, customer data, and more from theft, fraud, and damage.

2. Organisational resilience

Technology plays an integral part in disaster recovery. An organisation must have the means and capacity for maintaining operations while coping with natural disasters. However, it is also key to adapting, adjusting, and aligning with new realities such as those that were created by the COVID-19 pandemic.

3. Cloud applications

Depending on the organisation's architecture and infrastructure, it can save millions by opting for Cloud computing. The Cloud allows organisations to eliminate the labour burden and expense of large Information Technology units. The Cloud lets organisations store, backup, access, and share information with speed and ease. It offers multiple business office and administrative functions, virtual meeting opportunities, and presentation tools in addition to the internet universe.

4. Systems integration

Technology produces individual systems, some of which are standardised, and most of which are unique to the organisation. Separate systems serve respective functionalities in Accounting, Human Resources, Operations, Logistics, Shipping & Handling, and more. The nature of the organisation may require a whole or partial connection between functionalities. For example,

Accounting needs access to some Human Resources data, Shipping & Handling and Logistics require integration, and so on. It is up to Information Technology to leverage, integrate, and secure these partnerships.

5. Social media

Technology has empowered multiple social media platforms. Organisations have a presence on Facebook, Instagram, Twitter, and many other channels. That image is both the one the organisation wants to convey and the one the public creates. It takes continuing and close monitoring to keep that social media presence authentic and favourable.

6. Assets management

Organisations consume resources, raw materials, and human capital. Executives have a continuing *need-to-know* regarding the asset inventory. They require real-time reports on the currency, deployment, and flow of assets, as well as the indicated trending.

7. CGRM

Corporate Governance and Risk Management (CGRM) must be integrated. According to The Organisation for Economic Cooperation and Development (OECD) reports,

> "*while risk-taking is a fundamental driving force in business and entrepreneurship, the cost of risk management failures is still often underestimated, both externally and internally, including the cost in terms of management time needed to rectify the situation.*

Corporate governance should, therefore, ensure that risks are understood, managed, and, when appropriate, communicated' (OECD, 2014).

Technology provides the means and methods to keep these interests aligned.

8. Infrastructure

All organisations depend on their architecture. They are built by design to function in specific ways. This framework includes core functions like human resources, operations, and marketing. Technology drives their respective needs and needs that span these functionalities to provide a cohesive unit.

9. Compliance data

Executive Leaders are personally charged with governance and compliance. Any organisation subject to compliance policy and regulation has multiple reports to maintain and deliver. Information Technology is key to data gathering, integration, and delivery.

10. Digital transformation

Advanced Technology does not permit executives time to stick with the technology they have. Accelerated technology makes the status quo static and obsolete. Executive Leaders must be tech-savvy enough to see what is happening and ensure their organisation remains at the forefront of the competition.

Executive Leaders are expected to face and resolve these challenges regularly. However, while these actions maintain the organisation's health, they do not advance their strategic growth. They provide little in terms of invention and innovation.

Invention and Innovation — Not the Same Thing

Both *Invention* and *Innovation* involve something new. However, they are not the same thing, and it is essential to distinguish one from the other.

- "Invention" refers to "the brand-new thing." *Entrepreneur's Encyclopedia* defines "Invention" as *"An object, process or technique that displays an element of novelty. In certain circumstances, legal protection may be granted to an invention by way of a patent"* (Invention, 2020).

  The iPhone, for instance, was a revolutionary Invention. Each of its many elements called for Invention. The iPhone upgrades regularly by adding new Inventions in terms of cameras, buttons, software, and more. However, most patented Inventions never make such a dynamic difference to the world.

- "Innovation" is a creative event that may or may not use inventions. *"Innovation is the process through which value is created and delivered to a community of users in the form of a new solution"* (Todhunter, 2009). This definition stresses what the created value delivers primarily to the users—not the innovative organisation.

  However, Invention is not necessary for Innovation. For example, shipping containerisation increased the freight a ship could carry—exponentially. It also lowered the cost to the provider and customer as it expanded global commerce. This Innovative use of existing freight containers and cranes also put millions of dockers out of work.

Innovation is usually disruptive. The printing press and personal computers were Inventions with disruptive innovative impact on society. Electric vehicles include Inventions, but their Innovation will disrupt employment for long-haul drivers. On the other hand, the Uber Innovation brought low-cost convenience to millions without requiring any hardware Invention.

The difference between Invention and Innovation is not crucial to Executive Leaders—unless they confuse them. Invention on its own may be helpful, but it does not usually create or change markets or the users who shop there.

Conversely, executives stand accountable for the impact of Innovation. The social contract expects them to create value that improves users' lives, and where they anticipate negative disruption, they have some obligation to mitigate the harm.

- Uber optimised the existing concept of taxis and ridesharing with high-quality smartphone apps and GPS technology. In doing so, they provided a utility the market wanted. However, they also spawned competition, disrupted union standards, and challenged local governance.

- Amazon remains the world's one-stop shopping centre because of its ability to pivot quickly to new conditions. To offset its growing labour burden and still fulfil its customer promise, Amazon created sponsor affiliations that shift the accountability for fast delivery and customer service to sponsored products.

- Zoom was not the first platform for holding meetings. However, COVID-19 increased its utility a thousandfold. Its relatively simple operation has appealed to millions of people wanting to connect during lockdowns. It used technologies previously popular with business meetings and leveraged them for education, health care, and remote work.

- Automotive engineers and manufacturers are pushing technology forward to create self-driving vehicles. Cars and trucks will include multiple inventions, but the leading producer will disrupt the market with innovative utilities, including fast charging, increased mileage, and smooth performance. They must please a market looking for handsome design, comfortable interiors, and reasonable pricing. However, these innovators have experience in disrupting legacy markets.

- Blockchain technology already exists, but it has not made a significant impact. A cloud-based, universal ledger—it serves markets interested in investing and trading crypto-currency. The public finds the technology difficult to understand, so its disruptive innovation only serves a few focused markets. However, its potential seems enormous.

- Robotics exploit multiple inventions specific to identified needs in manufacturing, research, surgery, and other fields. Artificial Intelligence stands to increase the capabilities and potential for disruption. The machines that can correct their errors or learn from their experience pose significant difficulties for end users, social ethics, and others concerned about AI's limits.

The Lack of Understanding about Technology

"*Consumers have become increasingly habituated to look for and want what's new, best, fastest, more convenient, or more fashionable, and to tire of products much more quickly*" (Greenwald, 2014). Consumers buy what they need to fulfil their sustenance needs: food, water, shelter, and so on. However, they get psychological satisfaction from buying things they want.

Consumers demand products, and the demand drives both the supply and the price. This drives the economy—in a nutshell. That economy fast becomes static without invention and innovation. Consumers demand something new and unique for use in their work, household, vehicle, entertainment, and other consumer goods.

Individual customers might, for instance, switch detergent brands because one introduces a new fragrance or ingredient. However, you will not find much invention or innovation there.

Likewise, consumers often do not notice how innovation changes their lives. The personal computer was an invention that millions purchased for its ability to play video games. Developments in related technology now surround our daily lives with shopping, education, business, social media, and tens of thousands of other applications. While the technology behind Virtual and Augmented Reality is impressive, Artificial Intelligence informs our daily lives.

Organisations use technology to produce products and services. They use technology to reach and secure customers. They use technology internally to run organisation functions. They use technology to research and develop new products and services. So, the public assumption that technology is pretty much limited to social media, gaming, and shopping apps is naïve.

Senior executives may not know enough about technology, how to use it, and how it can affect their organisation performance and goals. However, they must embrace technology to:

1. **Create** critical points of difference between your product/service and the competition.

2. **Offer** customers solutions to their actual or perceived needs with a fresh, engaging, and satisfying customer experience.

3. **Compete** in new or niche markets.

4. **Secure** customer loyalty with products/services that exceed expectations.

Technology is so diverse in Invention and Innovation most executives do not fully grasp its workings. Nonetheless, they should know what they need to know about technology and their organisation, and Executive Leaders should know when and where they need advice.

Leveraging Technology in the Organisation

"In this rapidly evolving digital age, it is unimaginable for a business to continue to remain relevant and sustainable without leveraging technology... technology has disrupted every single aspect of our lives. Hence, as boundaries between buyers and

sellers dissolve and businesses expand across geographical borders, perhaps the only way to stay competitive is to adopt technology to its fullest and, sometimes, even find new uses for it" (Das, 2019).

The role of technology will vary significantly from one organisation to another. Organisations do not need the same technologies, nor do they need all that is new in technology. However, if they can enter the marketplace, grow there, meet their goals, and surpass their expectations, they must leverage the relevant technologies to change and succeed in a digitalised world. For instance, the transformative innovation they call "blockchain" may or may not have any beneficial role in your organisation.

All organisations must optimise the technology devices and applications that will:

1. Accelerate and reduce internal administrative functions.

For example, Human Resources can make strategic contributions once technology relieves it of clerical tasks. Technology will reduce its paperwork, improve employee communication, and enforce compliance concerns.

2. Improve the quantity and quality of operations.

A manufacturing organisation might introduce machines, monitors, and metrics to enhance its production. Information systems can integrate data from multiple critical points to analyse the performance of devices and people.

3. **Strengthen customer relationships.**

Sales and Marketing benefit from improved and real-time customer information. Organisations can integrate Customer Relationship Management (CRM) to customer retention, customer service, and shipping/handling/logistics functions.

4. **Enhance consumer experience.**

Many organisations do not sell products or services to the broader public. Nonetheless, they should optimise the available technology to inform the public, confirm their values, and share their transparency.

5. **Identify and recruit talent.**

Organisations require a pipeline of high-potential performers. Technology can help locate the talent, engage their interest, and cultivate relationships that last into employment.

Technology does not replace the need for talented Executive Leaders. Organisations' tech-knowledgeable leaders know enough about technology to see its values and find the experts to advise, design, and execute their technology needs.

Best Tech Practices

"Leveraging technology" means using technology resources, tools, and know-how to advance the organisation.

> *"This is not the first time in history that innovation and technology have fundamentally changed the way we live*

and work. But it is the first time we've been exposed to change at this scale and speed" (Otero, 2019).

This future shock has been overwhelming the average person since before the turn of this century. People under 40 have been born into and matured within this ecosystem.

However, there are some things you must remember about technology:

- **It is not neutral.** It bears the bias and interest of its creators. So, while it may affect human life, it may not be for the better. Social media, for example, have changed the way people live and communicate. However, the technologies that make this social communication possible also profit from the social traffic while risking your identity and other personal information. The platform creators have been less than transparent about their strategy and operation.

- **It is not absolute.** Technology must evolve continuously; it cannot stand still. So, there is no "gold standard," no "one-size-fits-all" tech portfolio for your organisation. Executive Leaders must educate themselves on the capabilities of different technology resources, tools, and applications if they hope to fulfil their decision-making obligations to their stakeholders.

- **It is not intuitive.** Technology still interacts with humans. So, the utilitarian value is a function of the users' ability to interact. While individuals may approach technology with different skill sets and earnest eagerness, they will need training. They not only need training in the technology's operation, but they also need the education to align this with organisational goals and values.

- **It is not innovation.** Technology is utilitarian. It becomes innovative through human decision to apply it in novel ways, hopefully improving the human experience.

Executives are tasked with three mandatory strategies: "*Run your business. Change your business. Reinvent your business*" (Otero, 2019). They must focus on technologies that ease, manage, and drive these tasks.

- **Recruit talent that differs from yours.**

  Do not hire on gut feelings. Hire talent that aligns with the organisation's purpose. Netflix has a policy where people expect to be released from employment when they no longer contribute to the company's advance. Even the Chief HR Officer who invented the policy terminated herself when she had accomplished her goals.

- **Create a culture that respects the diversity of talent and insights.**

  It takes diverse views and inputs to invent and reinvent. However, it takes a culture that enables and empowers such contributions in a psychologically safe, no-fear environment.

- **Organise a *Futures Team*, a team commissioned with a focus on reorganizing and reinventing.**

A Futures Team must resist satisfaction with the status quo, business as usual, and "just the way things are." This *Futures Team* is peopled with those who are excited by anticipation and adaptation. Technology in all its forms provides the means and methods to design the organisation's presence as markets change.

- **Involve stakeholders from all functional silos and all levels of hierarchies.**

  Stakeholders include rank and file hourly workers, board members, customers, outside experts and advisors, and Executive Leaders. Each person in each position must understand and value the technologies with which they interact.

- **Develop evolving IT leadership.**

  A young organisation places great hands-on work in front of its Information Technology directors. However, as organisations grow, they must advance with respect for their strategic value. Their leaders require the information and guidance for leveraging technology into their future.

  Without this energy and direction, "*most companies realize the importance of innovation, but they struggle with knowing how to deploy, use and integrate innovation to achieve their strategic priorities*" (Duval, 2019).

  Getting there is a problem. The media buzz with news of trends in Big Data, Artificial Intelligence, Robotics, and Digitisation. Whether any or all of this is important to you or your organisation, it may mean identifying existing strengths and weaknesses. It most certainly means you need critical input to describe your present situation and coach you on your future.

- **Big Data** refers to the vast amount of data gathered by and accessible to organisations. It describes a resource so extensive that it challenges users to use it wisely and effectively.

  Big Data requires transmission and storage capacities that decision makers must understand if they are to optimise the data for their focused markets and purpose. It is Big Data that has moved so many operations to the Cloud.

- **Artificial Intelligence (AI)** confuses many, especially those threatened by radical imaginations. AI dates to the 1950s when it was used to solve complex problems. You recognise it today in Siri, Alexa, and other technologies that mimic human memory and processing.

  Machine Learning allows computer-assisted drafting and manufacturing robots to "learn" from their repetitive functions, revising their processes to correct errors. *Deep Learning* takes it further as machines learn without direction and supervision. Deep Learning mines the unlabelled data to create algorithms without human participation.

- **Robotics** make manual work more manageable, more accurate, and more cost-effective. Robots now assemble cars, pick/pull products from inventories, and perform challenging surgeries. Organisations will pursue robotics applications because of the direct and indirect benefits.

Robots, nonetheless, alter the working relationship between leaders and their employees. They work without negligence or fault, but they also work without personality or sense of community. Dependency on robotics also sacrifices the benefits of diversity and collaboration.

- **Digitisation** transforms analogue material—photos, videos, recordings, documents, and more—into coded formats for computer process, transmit, and store. *Digitalisation* uses that technology to build business models, reimagine processes, and optimise value-added opportunities.

Digital transformation reconfigures today's organisations, integrating digitalisation to help organisations deal with customer-driven change. It makes change a core value and competency and requires agile thinking and management.

Here's Your Takeaway

Executive Leaders must understand the difference between Innovation and Invention. Customer experience, competition, and scalable growth depend on the optimisation of both.

Invention gives an organisation an edge, a unique and novel attraction. However, Executive Leaders must leverage existing and emerging technologies to improve, make, and move inventive products and services. Technocrats do not lead most organisations, but Executive Leaders need enough familiarity and experience with technology to make informed decisions regarding tech needs, tools, and strategies.
They should:

- Distinguish between Invention and Innovation,
- Face the challenges presented by technology, and
- Implement best practices in technology tools and strategies.

Chapter 8: Operations Strategy and Organisational Optimisation

Here's What to Expect

- ✓ Understand optimisation
- ✓ Avoid hurdles to optimisation
- ✓ Jump hurdles to optimisation
- ✓ Design solutions
- ✓ Maximise integration

One of the biggest mistakes an organisation can make is to confuse *Operations Strategy* and *Operational Management.* The latter deals with day-to-day management, while Operations Strategy is a longer-term view of how the organisation strategically manages its resources and processes. *Organisational*

Optimisation is only effective when aligned to Operations Strategy and the end customer.

Many organisations struggle with this concept, and in many cases, they focus on one aspect of Operations Strategy and optimise that alone. The critical question every organisation needs to ask: "Is the digital transformation about the company or the customer?" If it is not about the customer, it is *not* an Operations Strategy and will not transform the organisation. It will only be about optimisation, and this will not shift the needle to stay ahead of the competition.

An Operations Strategy must:

1. **Encompass** the overall direction of the organisation from the executive leadership.
2. **Build** long-term operations capability.
3. **Meet** the needs of its customers.
4. **Learn** from day-to-day operational experience.

There will always be tension between these four components; however, organisations that build longer-term capability aligned to their customers' future needs will achieve a competitive advantage over their competitors and enable transformation more efficiently.

Competitor and customer behaviour can be irrational and unpredictable. Therefore, an ongoing alignment between the executive leadership team and those on the ground who manage day-to-day operations is critical to making the correct operations strategy decisions. This continuous cycle of alignment is also a crucial ingredient for optimising an organisation's resources and processes.

"Optimisation" and "maximisation" are used so frequently they risk the loss of meaning. For most people, "optimisation" refers to getting the biggest bang for your buck.

However, in contemporary organisations throughout a digitised culture, "Optimisation" has come to mean the art of making the best decisions in a world increasingly deep in mathematics, computer science, software, and algorithms. Multiple, complex, and challenging tools increase decision-making opportunities while confounding the many who seek to choose wisely. This confusion is one sign of Alvin Toffler's *Future Shock* (Random House, 1970), that psychological stress incurred as information, technology, career, and more overwhelm you. Choices have multiplied exponentially; this requires you to make "right" decisions with a higher degree of difficulty and at accelerated frequency.

For this development,

> *"Organizational Optimization is the new way to look at your organization, assess its current health and optimise its future potential. Its purpose is to strategically align the organization, optimise the execution of its strategy, and culturally set the stage for growth and prosperity"* (Hutcherson, 2014).

In some ways, too much is expected of Executive Leaders. However, they cannot have expertise in all areas. Organisation Operations and Operations Strategy call for some specialisation. A paint manufacturer, for instance, will operate differently than a dairy. Those same Executive Leaders must make the decisions necessary to find the talent capable of optimising their respective operations. They must know what they want the organisation to achieve and how to collaborate with operations talent to actualise this transformation.

Here's My Story

In working with an executive leader in an enterprise ICT company it became apparent quite quickly that there was an overarching ambition to have a more effective and efficient operations strategy. Nevertheless, the constant firefighting of issues and backdrop of multiple inflight single view initiatives prevented a cross functional collaboration across the organisation to uplift the capability and move the focus to Objectives and Key Results (OKR's).

I was engaged to help facilitate an external point of view with respect to how the organisation manages the customer experience at the front line and the flow on effect. I helped the leadership team to set up a model that brought together the right experts across the whole of business over a variety of collaboration sessions to ask the right questions and develop the insights from the learnings of the front-line staff, building long term partnerships and meeting the constant changing needs of their customers.

All specific measures of KPI's across business units were discussed and there was a clear alignment on moving towards an 'outcome based' partnership model with the respective partners. This model would incentivise the partners to work towards 'win/win' outcomes. Moreover, this type of operational strategy had the key ingredients of focusing on outcomes and transforming the customer experience in a way that was never attempted before. This established the foundation for game changing customer experiences.

Toward an Understanding of Optimisation

Understanding and executing organisational optimisation can challenge unfamiliar executives. Recent reports show 85 percent of executive decision makers believe digital transformation will play a strategic role in the coming years.

> "*However, only about 34 percent of companies have undergone some sort of digital transformation. This leaves about two-thirds of organizations that have not yet adopted any digital transformation strategies. Those that do not adopt such strategies will fall behind and risk losing revenue*" (New book teaches..., 2020).

The concept of optimisation of operations and organisations can be a lot to get your hands around. There is that casual understanding that organisations must stay current with evolving skills, processes, and market demands. However, globalisation and accelerating technology make decisions on such matters more complicated.

Optimisation presses organisation leaders to make critical decisions to the economy, efficiency, and effectiveness of performance:

- **Economy:** An organisation performs with *economy* when it spends less on the inputs and resources used.

- **Efficiency:** An organisation works with *efficiency* when there is a positive connection between the resources used and the outputs produced.

- **Effectiveness:** An organisation achieves *effectiveness* when its outcomes narrow the gap between intention and actualisation.

Organisational optimisation seeks to align all organisation's people, functions, and stakeholders with the intended customer experience. It aims to correlate those systems with social and environmental obligations as well. However, Operational Optimisation focuses more on operations and processes, a desire to expedite product and service performance without losing resources, energy, and costs. (For convenience and clarity, this chapter treats Operational Optimisation and Organisational Optimism as the same issue.)

Economy involves:

- Defining material, mechanical, and human resources.

- Developing strong relationships with resource providers.

- Building a logistics infrastructure to secure supply chains.

- Collaborating on Key Performance Indicators (KPIs) installed at critical process pain points.

Efficiency involves:

- Measuring gaps among resources used, resources rejected, and resources wasted.

- Identifying people, places, or processes accountable for losses.

- Using cost management skills to maximise the use of current assets and seek possible cost reductions.

- Monitoring individual and team performance against actual outcomes.

Effectiveness involves:

- Evaluating customer experience and satisfaction.

- Identifying the quality and quantity of outcomes.

- Adapting new skills and procedures to evolving markets.

- Improving performance, practices, and procedures to close identified gaps.

Overall, you must understand how operational optimisation serves organisational optimisation by creating a culture where continuous self-improvement is expected and effective.

Avoiding Hurdles to Optimisation

Optimisation is not static. It must be organic and dynamic, fluid and flexible. It requires repeated ideation and resolution. However, executive decision makers will face problems in making it happen.

1. Managing Overhead:

Overhead is an unstable variable. It includes scores of expenses not limited to facility rental and maintenance, equipment and equipment depreciation, multiple insurance policies and utilities, and much more.

> *"In general, overhead is defined as anything that does not include direct labor, direct materials, or expenses billed directly to the customer. Think of it as the expenses you are more or less stuck with, even if no business is coming in"* (Barstow, 2019).

Traditionally, orders will come down from the executive suite, directing everyone to cut costs. Some interpret this as an order to lay off people and reduce administrative costs. Such a narrow understanding of budgets drives unnecessary and irrelevant cuts. However, organisations now use *Overhead Value Analysis.*

Overhead Value Analysis differs "*by making both the managers who incur the costs (suppliers) and those who benefit from them (receivers or demanders) responsible for identifying which costs to cut*" (Neuman, 1975). This analytic process brings managers from throughout the hierarchy together to see what they have in common in terms of wants, needs, and providers. It encourages them to negotiate cost revisions related to sustaining customer outcomes.

Moreover, management will find considerable savings by digitising supply chains. Organisations miss opportunities when they continue to use labour, time, and paper-intensive supply chain processes. Digitisation is a tool and methodology that enables just-in-time inventories, economies of scale, and real-time transactions that save money.

2. Measuring Performance:

• Key Performance Indicators (KPI)

Every organisation performs differently, even those in the same economic sector. Measuring performance, therefore, is not standardised easily.

Each organisation must discern its most beneficial KPIs. For instance, KPIs for Sales might include sales per day, dollar per sales, and the percentage of contacts converted to sales. KPIs for professional services might consist of the number of clients served per month, billable hours collected per quarter, and results of customer satisfaction surveys.

Many organisations continue linking compensation to workers' incremental performance checks at 90 days, six months, and annually. However, contemporary organisations have moved away from those legacy practices toward more holistic approaches.

The Australian Industry Group explains these indicators should be part of a broader strategic performance cycle.

> "*The performance management cycle involves more than an annual review or appraisal meeting. It should be based on a continuous cycle, including the setting of objectives, the development of capabilities to achieve those objectives, facilitated by constant feedback, coaching and mentoring, and at least one formal review or appraisal meeting. Many organisations will also link their reward and recognition process to the performance management cycle*" (Introduction to the performance management cycle, 2014).

Designing and deploying such strategies requires executives to become deeply involved in understanding the roles that people fill within the organisation. They must develop those roles to align with the organisation's purposes and then recruit talent that fits those roles. Leaders should respect their associates for their capabilities and potentialities rather than by the knowledge, skills, and abilities found on resumes.

Individual executives may depend on metrics reporting on critical functions. They may prefer to see those KPIs in summary format or short-listed as needed. However, they should develop a culture where performance monitoring and assessment is a continuous process. People benefit from understanding their respective paths to individual success, and the organisation benefits from integrating those individual paths into a large fabric of success.

- **Objectives and Key Results (OKRs)**

Contemporary organisations emphasise collaboration. They set and monitor Objectives and Key Results (OKRs). These OKRs include robust challenges and stretch goals to engage teams, promote their collaboration, and align their productivity.

OKRs differ from KPIs because they do not measure individual worker performance. They are not static because they remain flexible enough to respond to evolving and stretch aspirations.

An *Objective* clarifies concrete, significant, and active targets. Objectives avoid theoretical, abstract, and unspecific goals. It answers the question. "What does this team (Unit, Department, etc.) want to accomplish?"

Key Results mark the steps toward the Objective. They mark specific, measurable, and verifiable actions along the path. Team leaders and Executive Leaders can observe and count these results with ease. Key Results answer the question, "What do we need to do to get there?"

Organisations typically assess the OKR achievement quarterly. That keeps objectives focused and at the front of the organisation's work. The OKRs become a framework for keeping people, teams, and management aligned with organisational goals.

Executive Leaders must work with teams to frame an overarching initiative with three to five Objectives. This sends a message throughout the organisation that these objectives have priority. Each Objective has three to five Key Results. These measures have the most precise targeted effect on the organisation's plan and purpose.

Leaders must articulate the OKRs in a language everyone understands. They also communicate the OKRs throughout the culture, so everyone understands their role in achieving or enabling the realisation of the OKRs.

Posting and sharing the Key Result Indicators puts the progress on the wall. An increasing number of organisations create a dashboard for monitoring the team's progress. They do so to encourage conversation and to drive stretch goals.

OKRs must target the customer. Every organisational effort must lead to the customer. Keeping the customer first avoids unnecessary and irrelevant work.

OKRs should be robust and ambitious. They must set aspirational positions. However, setting specific Key Results ties the ambition and aspiration to achievable impacts.

3. **Managing Risk:**

Organisations face multiply risks requiring senior management. Executive Leaders remain accountable for the prevention and resolution of threats at multiple levels. For the sake of clarity, you can focus on the following:

- **Safe Work:** Government regulation requires organisations to ensure continuing compensation for their employees who have suffered physical and psychological damages from their work and develop frameworks for returning to work.

  Safe Work Australia (SWA), Organisational Safety and Health Standards (OSHA), or their equivalent mandates specific safety requirements for different industries reflecting their respective physical risks from equipment, materials, toxins, carcinogens, and much more.

- **AASB, IFRS, GAAP (or its equivalent):** Australian Accounting Standards Board (AASB), International

Financial Reporting Standards (IFRS), and Generally Accepted Accounting Practices (GAAP) offers examples of best practices in financial reporting.

- **ISO (International Operations Standards):** The ISO and numerous equivalents offer detailed and demanding production standards for many manufacturing fields. The intent establishes internationally accepted quality norms.

- **Equity:** Various governments have established norms for the equitable employment of women, minorities, and other underserved or population marginalised groups.

Compliance with regulations is triggered and enforced by report, inspection, audit, and subsequent penalties and fines. Focused Executive Leaders want to avoid negative results because of the cost, disruption, and harm to organisation members, reputation, and goals.

Until an organisation moves to create a culture of transparency, autonomy, digitised processing, systems integration, and data analytics, this work remains repetitive, burdensome, and costly in terms of time, people, and resources.

Jumping Hurdles to Optimisation

These preventive management strategies help organisations navigate the rough waters around them. However, some measures offer a more positive framework:

1. **Reduce organisational inefficiency:**

"Organizational efficiency is the organization's degree of success in using the least possible inputs in order to produce the highest possible outputs" (Li). Organisations might use raw materials, data, people, and more without achieving the highest possible output.

Inefficient meetings, processes, and communications cost organisations billions, costs felt as losses by all stakeholders. So, executives must seek solutions for the waste they know about—or should know about. Their option is to optimise their organisation's status as a digitised centre.

2. **Redesign supply chains:**

Organisations should master their supply chains instead of leaving the logistics to providers. They need systems that recognise, report, and revise adverse incidents. Systems must detect lapses or inaccuracies and then continue positive correction.

3. **Reimagine Information Technology:**

Executive Leaders must empower a culture where information technology managers have value well beyond their role as designers, implementers, and data collectors. Information Management is much more than a systems helpdesk and data processing centre.

Leaders must maximise technology's potential in strategic partnership with analytics, forecasting, customer profiling, and other keys to efficient productivity. The comprehensive reboot of IT may be beyond the knowledge, skill, and ability of most executives, so they should reach out for advice from experienced and focused consultants.

4. Resolve inconsistencies:

Organisations pursue growth, and growth disrupts the status quo. Nonetheless, Executive Leaders want to maintain a consistent dynamic because investors and other stakeholders worry when they observe volatility. Executives find it easier to maintain that balance if their strategic decisions remain aligned with the organisation's purpose.

For example, processes will run inconsistently across the organisation. They may run at different speeds across different departments, duplicate work and effort, or even contribute little to the desired outputs. Digitisation, however, can detect, disclose, and resolve these problems. Moreover, the self-improvement resulting from iterative cycles will reduce the potential for prolonged or future inconsistencies.

Digitisation describes not only inconsistent behaviours but also prescribes corrective measures with real-time reporting to authorised personnel. Without it, an analysis of gathered documentation delays response and resolution for weeks.

5. Master cost control and cost reduction:

Cost Control differs from Cost Reduction, although they both improve organisational efficiency.

- *Cost Control* reveals whether actual overall costs align with budgeted costs and where variances occur. It is a typical organisational process to manage the total costs of a process. Any organisation should work to keep its cost from going beyond the budget.

Cost Control begins with a thorough budgeting process. A casually prepared budget only invites cost overruns. Executive Leaders must immerse themselves in the process because they will be accountable for costs. Obviously, they require accurate and immediate reporting on organisational performance to recognise and heal the pain points.

- *Cost Reduction* seeks to lower the cost of unit production without sacrificing quality. Effective Cost Reduction monitors production to identify the waste of resources and eliminate unnecessary steps in the production chain of events.

  Only comprehensive digitisation provides real-time information on multiple tiers in any process. It observes and analyses the value of materials, designs, decisions, and outputs against intended quality and cost per unit.

The preceding behaviours describe decisive methods of optimising organisations and their operation. However, there is no Standard Operating Procedure. There is no standard "off-the-shelf solution." Organisations are unique, and their Executive Leaders need the support of consulting services and Trusted Advisors willing and able to customise their assistance.

Other Solutions

Depending on the size, nature, and goals of an organisation, it may pursue other options when optimising its performance, operation, and purpose.

1. Outsourcing:

"Outsourcing is a business practice in which services or job functions are farmed out to a third party. In information technology, [for instance] an outsourcing initiative with a technology provider can involve a range of operations, from the entirety of the IT function to discrete, easily defined components, such as disaster recovery, network services, software development or QA testing" (Overby, 2017).

Organisations often outsource payroll, customer service, and other back-office functions. Outsourcing has the benefit of reducing the direct labour burden and securing expertise otherwise unavailable within the organisation.

Outsourcing piece work and administrative tasks relieve the organisation to focus on revenue-producing and value-added strategic activities.

However, organisations must find a beneficial balance between outsourcing and insourcing. They must be agile and flexible enough to pivot under pressure or in crisis. For example, COVID-19 has disabled many departments. Organisations dependent on outsourced functions like customer service, reservations, and other call centres found those services paralysed by absenteeism and leadership loss at the time of the pandemic.

2. Customer-Centric Culture:

A customer-centric culture marks the most successful organisations where they practice customer-centricity horizontally and vertically throughout the organisation infrastructure. They focus sharply on creating and sustaining a unique customer experience from before to after the consumer transaction.

A customer-centric culture creates a context and an environment for customer interest, satisfaction, and loyalty. This takes more than a claim that customers are the top priority. Only digitisation will enable organisations to recognise valuable customer prospects, monitor their contacts and transactions, and analyse customer feedback.

Customer-centric cultures find customers are the source of dense information other than their purchase. Customer data is rich with information about customer behaviour even when they do not purchase. In new markets, organisations must monitor their behaviour characteristics on multiple social media channels as well as their decision to buy or not buy. Digitisation helps to establish and sustain lifelong customer relationships.

3. Futures Forecasting:

Legacy organisations have long relied on the human ability to gather, archive, and integrate data before forecasting trends to support decision-making. However, *The Economist* asserts, *"Machines are replacing humans in prediction and planning"* (Digitisation is helping to deliver goods faster, 2019).

Deep-learning algorithms, artificial intelligence, and advanced supply chain software have moved trending, forecasting, and predictability beyond the reach of manual efforts. In doing so, digitisation has improved pricing, accelerated delivery, and redirected logistics. *"Digitisation will have the impact on supply chains that steam and electricity had on manufacturing"* (Digitisation is helping ..., 2019).

3. Process Re-engineering:

The capacity for discerning patterns in an organisation's data produces Information. Until recently, the quality of the Information depended on the quantity of data. The more data available, the easier it was to make decisions.

However, shifting to digitisation expands that capacity enormously. One advantage lies in its recognition of process issues. The ability to interpret large databases includes identifying process pain points; that is, critical points may reveal duplicate work, consistent human or machine error, and other problems. The data reports in real time, so management can respond quickly and confidently to re-engineer the process.

4. Lean Organisation:

The reduced structure of a "Lean" organisation eliminates any activities that do not add value to the organisation's outputs.

Lean organisations show their commitment to reducing waste. By eliminating levels of management, they also reduce communication, paperwork, and authority issues. The Lean hierarchy encourages collaboration with direct horizontal and vertical communication.

Digitisation empowers and drives the resulting organisational energy and helps Lean organisations respect Lean suppliers as reliable resources. Today's high-demand economy increases the pressure on organisations to step up and design Lean futures.

5. Innovative Thinking:

Tomorrow's Executive Leaders understand that digitisation is a necessary part of an economy obsessed with innovation. They see how the optimisation of digitisation has spurred economic growth. Like those in automation and Artificial Intelligence, evolving and competing technologies have increased and intensified the quality and volume of Big Data. They have accelerated productivity, inventory turnover, logistics, financial accounting, and more.

Executive Leaders have come to realise that Digital Natives have the talents that drive the future. Business media have been obsessed with Millennials and how difficult they are to manage. However, the "Digital Natives" who belong to that generation will shape and drive an optimised future.

Their contributions will alter the face of retail, accelerate delivery, facilitate manufacturing assembly, and expand pharmaceuticals' research and global reach. They understand that *"most digital technologies provide* possibilities *for efficiency gains and customer intimacy. However, if people lack the right mindset to change and the current organizational practices are flawed, DT [Digital Transformation] will simply magnify those flaws*" (Tabrizi, Lam, et al., 2019).

They must define the targets digitisation can solve, define the outcomes desired, explore internal and external solutions, and adopt and adapt means and practices enabled and empowered by technology.

They find support for that mindset with a pivot toward Design Thinking and Agile Thinking:

- **Design Thinking:**

  "*Design Thinking is an iterative process in which we seek to understand the user, challenge assumptions, and redefine problems in an attempt to identify alternative strategies and solutions that might not be instantly apparent with our initial level of understanding. At the same time, Design Thinking provides a solution-based approach to solving problems. It is a way of thinking and working as well as a collection of hands-on methods*" (Dam & Teo, 2020).

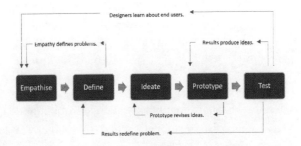

Figure 8.1: A Basic Iterative Process

Despite the appearance in Figure 8.1, it is important to note this is a non-horizontal iterative process. It intends to be disruptive, and it depends on the readiness of data.

- **Agile Thinking:**

  Mandated Agile Principles[2] support nimble, innovative, and improvisational responses to design and development needs. The pioneers of Agile approaches

  > *"aspired to create workplaces that allowed the human spirit to soar, that created meaning and joy, that drew on everyone's creative talents, that allowed people to live, to eat, to drink, to work and to indulge in a thousand and one acts without which people wither and die, all the while in workplaces that are highly productive and profitable"* (Denning, 2017).

  This mindset has become a prominent force in contemporary management. It respects the collaboration of diverse talents, capabilities, and insights to expedite the decisions necessary to economical, efficient, and effective outputs.

  If you think of a rugby game, you understand each player has an assigned task and a designated area of the field. However, you also appreciate the team's victory depends on quick thinking and agile movement, the

---

[2] The Mandated Agile Principles arose from The Agile Manifesto authored by a group of software intellectuals gathered in 2001 as a framework for future collaboration.

strategic interplay of athletes that positions them for the shot on goal.

Agile thinking emphasises the dynamic and fluid flow of the process. Illustrations like Figure 8.2 feature curves or loops that return to the cycle with new or revised information. The cycle generates smaller cycles or Scrums

Figure 8.2: Basic Agile Cycle

that solve arising issues with ad hoc independence and collaboration. Illustrations of Agile cycles often include gears to illustrate the connectivity and integration of clock-like mechanisms.

Agile frameworks have proven highly effective in overcoming the challenges facing today's Executive Leaders. It has increased their capabilities and strengthened their resilience.

- **Accelerate:**

  " We cannot ignore the daily demands of running an organisation, which traditional hierarchies and managerial processes can still do very well. What they do not do well is identify the most important hazards and opportunities early enough, formulate creative strategic initiatives nimbly enough, and implement them fast enough" (Kotter, 2012).

The Agile culture enables speedy attention and resolution—not for the sake of speed. It engages more associates in the action. Teams lead with their heart, will, and remarkably valuable diversity of skills, insights, and talents. It forms coalitions and cohorts across functional silos and significantly increases ownership in outcomes.

- **Align:**

  Customer satisfaction is the priority of Agile approaches. Agility optimises iterations, rotating cycles through planning, analysis and design, testing, and evaluation. The cycle repeats continuously—carrying forward the lessons learned.

  If new challenges arise during the reiteration, Agile management permits the creation of a sub-assignment to attack that outlier difficulty. The problem is handled with speed by a Scrum, an ad hoc team chosen for their relevant experience and skills.

  Keeping these multiple activities and cross-functional experiences aligned can be difficult without committed, solid leadership at the top. The recommended standard for alignment is the corporate vision.

- **Learn:**

  To keep Agile behaviour fresh and innovative, the participants must continue to learn. Executive

Leaders must create and maintain a culture of learning. From the top down, the organisation must encourage and facilitate risk-taking and mistake-making as well as training and development.

Digital technology makes this easier, too. Intelligent approaches to training with videos, remote learning, and mentoring can compound the learning results and shorten learning time. Organisations are best positioned to select and build a curriculum serving their organisation and customer needs.

- **Predict:**

  Agile teams do not function in a vacuum. They must take advantage of the bountiful data available. Given the breadth and depth of data resources, they must have skills in discerning the values and relevance.

Teams need metrics on their own performance to remain focused, purposeful, and efficient. They need enough current and historical data to make algorithms operative and informative. There are statistical models to forecast probabilities, models that begin to learn from themselves as they are fed additional relevant data. Even the team thinking—that values diverse individual contributions—must still make data-based decisions.

Adding Value by Reimagining Risk Management

Legacy organisations and management thinking considered Risk Management a necessary evil because Risk Management costs them money with little apparent investment return.

Social and worker demands forced changes, and in the mid-20th century, organisations realised that expenditures on workplace safety could offset lost time and productivity.

Although many employers proceeded with reluctance to aggressively reduce risk, federal legislatures created agencies to define and enforce safety.

However, organisations have developed more complexly, and "risk" now covers much more than the factory "slip-and-fall" accidents of the past.

- **Physical risk**

    Executive Leaders have accepted that protecting and preventing worker injury has a priority. Concerns about productivity, lost time and experience, and litigation have driven this acceptance. For example, safety audit results will affect the cost of insurance.

    Whatever the motives, employee safety has improved. It still takes leadership to model compliance and respect for the Risk Management policies and procedures.

    As the nature of work has changed, physical risks have changed, too. Where employees were once exposed to heavy lifting and toxic materials, many physical problems now arise from repetitive office work. Moreover, during the

COVID-19 pandemic workers feared returning to a workplace where they could expose themselves to COVID-19 or its mutations.

Executive Leaders would do well to understand their organisation's physical work fully. They should invest in precautions and equipment to reduce the quantity and severity of injuries. Moreover, they must commit all managers to support offensive and defensive safety routines.

- **Mental risk**

  Employee claims of mental stress did not arise until late in the 20th-century. They are also hard to prevent because they can be challenging to define. Because such claims are individual, they provide little in terms of symptomology or standards of diagnosis.

  Add the emergence of such claims to an increasingly litigious society, and employers can be vulnerable. Nevertheless, such claims can be genuine, damaging, and expensive.

  Executive Leaders cannot let their Risk Management guard down. They must launch robust response frameworks to address mental stress signs: absenteeism, fatigue, chronic depression, disengagement, and withdrawal. Organisations may not be responsible for individual workers' addiction and dependency issues; however, it remains in employers' and employees' interest to collaborate on therapy and resolution.

  The radical impact of the COVID-19 pandemic and the subsequent work diaspora have impacted organisations heavily. Statistics showed increases in depression, addiction, and suicide related to the lockdowns. Moreover, many workers sent home to work found it difficult to adapt to the altered work environment.

Some reported being overwhelmed by working in an environment with children who also needed help with online schooling and with spouses newly unemployed as employers shut down. They also reported burnout with virtual meetings and loss of workplace relationships.

These new contexts have taxed employers, too. They found existing Employee Assistance Programs (EAPs) have been passive. That is, employee participation with EAPs has been voluntary, often not much more than a referral. However, workers and their work were showing multiplying concerns.

Executive Leaders must assess how their organisations handle these emerging issues and accelerate their response mechanics. Employers have tasked managers to improve their skills in empathy, active listening, and communication. They must keep employees engaged, sustain the corporate culture, and remind workers that they impact the customer experience.

- **Intelligence risk**

  Technology has empowered employers and employees with extraordinary capabilities. Optimised digitisation drives the global economy. It differentiates the success and growth of one organisation from another. However, it has also created tangible threats.

Employees have access to large quantities of quality information. It makes organisations vulnerable to the theft, exploitation, and compromise of corporate information assets. Employees have stolen important data, patents, and customer resources for profit or spite. Employers must update and monitor their legal protections against the abuse or misuse of the organisation's intellectual information.

However, cybercrime has become the biggest threat to organisations. Individuals, competitors, and governments have compromised databases' integrity at governments, hospitals, political parties, and corporations worldwide. They have stolen the data for profit, held the data for ransom, damaged the organisation's ability to operate, or stolen clients, customers, and members' identities. The most sophisticated cybersecurity assets have proven vulnerable to hacking, sometimes at the hand of foreign enemies.

Executive Leaders must assess their organisation's vulnerability now and into the future. They must determine how well they are equipped to reduce or eliminate the risk. However, this risk requires constant scrutiny and may need the help of a Trusted Advisor to set up the defence and monitor the offence.

Executive Leaders moving from another organisation, transitioning to a more responsible position, or driving their organisation's transformation must consider risk in a new way during these volatile times. Risk Management was once left to Human Resources to distribute policies and procedures and to discipline those who violated the rules. The emerging organisation faces new threats and demands requiring more decisive action from the top down.

Today and tomorrow, organisations need Executive Leaders to appreciate and respect the potential of risk and its cost to the organisation and its people.

Optimisation Requires Integration

In optimised organisations, these systems work interdependently. Each approach is unique and has its tools and methodologies. However, each of them maximises the performance and effect of others. They require senior executives to adopt a more holistic approach to management.

Senior executives often lock into a functional role in finance, operations, marketing, or otherwise. Their focus on revenue and earnings pushes them to reductionist thinking, strict rational concepts that prove reductionist. They approach all elements and processes as links in chains.

Holism asks Executive Leaders to envision all things as dynamic, fluid, and organic. In this vision, each item has a connection to all other items, making decisions more challenging. Each decision has a broader and faster impact. To succeed, Executive Leaders must embrace solutions that work with other transformation components to help them meet their strategic goals.

Executive Leaders must wrestle with multilayered decisions always. They work at the nexus of multiple factors and forces, making their choices demanding and solutions difficult to discern. Digitisation presents the latest challenge. It is not easy to understand, and it takes experts to strategise and launch.

However, the solutions examined here should optimise the organisation to bring them closer to the end customer so the organisation can serve them more effectively and efficiently. Digitisation is key to transforming an organisation into a climate and culture that reduce or eliminate barriers, sustains preventive measures, and supports holistic visions in making strong, data-based, results-based moves.

Here's Your Takeaway

Evolving organisations face yet another challenge. The nature of work that you can expect to change is doing so at an accelerated pace. It is unsettling and confusing.

Organisations with the resources to do so will stay the course and navigate the choppy waters of outside pressures. However, Executive Leaders must provide direction to more satisfactory, engaging, and productive work suited to still unknown evolving contexts.

The necessary optimisation requires Executive Leaders who are ready to transition wholly:

- Introduce and model new strategic and infrastructure thinking.
- Mandate co-collaborative work and integration.
- Align policy and process with organisation goals.
- Add value to a customer-centric focus.

Section 3

Chapter 9: The Future of Work

Here's What to Expect

- ✓ Dealing with a digital future
- ✓ What to learn from the See Change underway
- ✓ Taking the critical path
- ✓ Overcoming challenges by the future of work

The world of work is changing, and the rate of change has accelerated. Organisational leaders know this, but they struggle to provide the day-to-day work experiences demanded by the distributed and decentralised work that for example resulted from the COVID-19 pandemic and other factors.

Peoples' experiences—customers and workers—will drive every organisation's competitive advantage. The rise of AI, machine learning, robotics, and other technologies will replace and assist workers in creating new organisational challenges.

Evolving technology will help workers find solutions to problems that would have been referred up the chain of command. For example, AI can suggest the next best actions for Customer Service agents, and devices like Google's second-generation work goggles allow employees to access training videos and instruction manuals with a simple tap to the temple.

Moreover, technology has made remote work easier and possible when necessary. "*The Australian Industry Group (2016) found that between 2014 and 2015, 32 percent of Australians undertook freelance work. Of these:*

- 44% was in web mobile software development.
- 14% in design & creative.
- 13% in customer & administration.
- 10% in sales & marketing.
- 8% in writing.

Together, this suggests that the gig economy is a small segment of the overall talent market, but being undertaken by and for large numbers of enterprises and individuals, in roles from basic to complex, and with a significant economic benefit" (Mills & Jan, 2017).

A more recent study by researchers from the University of Adelaide, Queensland University of Technology, and the University of Technology Sydney found:

- Over 15 percent of those surveyed considered their gig work as an essential part of their income.

- Over 24 percent considered it important but not essential.

- City-dwelling young males are more likely to work remotely.

- Gig workers on digital platforms like the flexibility of the work — but not the compensation (Revealing the True Size ..., 2019).

This shift from permanent staff to gig workers or freelancers poses a threat to an organisation's talent base, net revenue, and customer experience. Executive Leaders must meet the challenge posed by a decentralised workforce when they have lost visual and verbal connection when their communities disperse.

They must also embrace the opportunity to reconsider what values they might find in Analytics, Cloud Computing, Blockchain Technology, and more. They must estimate the cost of new technologies and the cost of not moving forward with emerging technologies.

When the workforce "disappears," as it were, legacy Organisation Charts lose their value. The span and scope of management shift dramatically. At this pain point, Executive Leaders have the resilience to pivot away from legacy formations to more fluid and flexible systems.

For instance, during pandemic lockdowns, Zoom (and similar technology) enabled individual and group meetings. This technology helped organisations to sustain some sense of connection and normalcy.

Many remote workers soon found they lacked confidence in using the virtual meeting platforms. However, this "negative" moment allows management leaders to reconfigure their training and development to facilitate communication. It empowers Executive Leaders to determine what technology fulfils their organisation's needs going forward.

Here's My Story

Working environments have changed and shifted from traditional office spaces with rigid working hours in restrictive cubicles to open plan, activity-based arrangements to 'working from anywhere' concepts.

It took a large enterprise organisation time to appreciate this new norm and realise the benefits of a remote workforce. The new norm is a world where automation, Artificial Intelligence, and other influences liberate employees from work's mundane tasks and physical limitations. The future of work allows for more focus on significant contributions to the community and a greater sense of purpose.

Organisations must focus on employee experiences driven by:

- Leveraging technology to gain real-time insights into their workforce,

- Monitoring workforce sentiment and employee wellbeing,

- Managing connections between leaders and teams in a work-from-anywhere environment; and

- Investing in training and development to help their workers grow and adapt in changing environments.

The new hybrid workforce is a challenge for everyone. However, employees need to be front and centre within the organisation, as the future of work is all about employee wellbeing. The employee experience is tightly coupled with authentic leadership and active listening to on-the-ground challenges.

Dealing with Digital

Both Executive Leaders and workers must come to terms with what "digitisation" means in real-world terms. It is not always understood easily. For example, digital watches have replaced analogue watches. They have replaced mechanical watches to the point where many people cannot tell time using the legacy systems. Likewise, contemporary people need instructions on how to use telephones with rotary dials.

However, digitisation also allows machines to compute rapidly, mimic human decisions, correct machine performance, communicate globally, and much more. It eliminates paperwork, expands storage, and speeds processing of all sorts. It validates, fixes, and ensures quality, and it reduces resource consumption and waste. In these ways, digitisation is crucial to future economies, existing and emerging industrial sectors, and social and environmental eco-systems.

Executives See Change

Executive Leaders must deal with considerable changes in front of them. They understand technology is pivotal in ensuring the customer remains at the heart of the organisation and company culture. They must remain current on the software and hardware that can make a difference. They must be able to cost, budget, and invest in the most effective technology for their organisation. However, they may require advice to narrow their options with the data and evidence to power their decisions.

Executive Leaders must explore accessible ventures in Analytics and Cloud-computing to optimise their digital operations, sophisticated and challenging concepts for many laypeople. They may increase vulnerabilities to cybersecurity and intellectual property. However, they are necessary expenses.

Globalisation and universal access to the internet and Cloud have overwhelmed many. Like everyone else, Executive Leaders must handle multilayered and accelerating decisions in a climate of *future shock*. They must lead organisations able to pivot as the winds change direction.

Executives will lead—or be led—by this transformation. They must master the future framework, infrastructure, strategy, technology, talents, and more. They must embrace the value of change; at the same time, they must mitigate disruptive damage. Understanding the *what* and *why* of future work should help leaders enable how work will change.

Workers See Change

With the advancement of analytics, work packages and assignments will be distributed to the most capable worker. Worker performance will be rated based on their quality of service and real-time feedback, whether from front-line staff or internal staff supporting other teams. However, only technology can integrate these elements.

The COVID-19 pandemic and related socio-economic disruptions have forced many organisations into enormous and fundamental structural change. Many have responded by sending work home with employees; others have increased the load on remote workers, and many organisations have decided to make distance work their *new norm*. As work is distributed and dispersed, organisations risk losing customer focus with workers out of sight and beyond supervisor observation and peer support.

The world of work evolves naturally. The issues of supply and demand change. New raw materials appear. Provider and consumer tastes mature. Engineers revise tools and systems. Patents expire, and innovations disrupt. These are the rhythms of the economy.

A sustaining, engaging, and satisfying customer experience journey demands organisations exploiting their intelligence, resilience, and agility to respond to needs arising from many quarters in this tumultuous climate.

Contemporary organisations build frameworks on the integration and leveraging of three competencies:

1. **Service:** Organisations need a deep Cloud foundation that enables and affects rapid and flexible responses to customer wants and needs. Groups must have the capability to please customers with their digital experience in answering, assessing, and fulfilling.

2. **Insights:** Advanced Analytics and Artificial Intelligence improve customer satisfaction, adding new dimensions to their shopping journey. Without in-person face-to-face meetings, the technology can still add context and texture to

the purchase with voice recognition and integrated feedback. Simultaneously, the interaction supplies organisations with new information and customer data to drive their emerging strategies.

3. **Workforce:** Executive Leaders must also respect that the new nature of the work experience has changed radically for their workers. They must leverage advanced technology to improve the work—and employees' perception of their work. For instance, relocating workers leaves them detached and unsupported unless executive leadership optimises technology to reduce their processes, improve real-time support, and design workers' work.

Historically, organisations have focused on their internal hierarchy and functional silos to streamline a chain of events that processed resources into deliverables. This focus on the speed and efficiency of operations too often came at the expense of customer satisfaction.

Well-informed customers, global competition, and advancing technology have strengthened buying intelligence and power. These factors have increased expectations for organisations to reimagine their customer and worker relationships to ensure sustainable and scalable quality. They must see the opportunity in arising threats.

The Critical Path

Technology makes Work-at-Home, Digital Nomads, Gig Workers, and other nontraditional work options possible. It will build on current examples' success because leveraging technology can anticipate the nature of change and shape the response.

1. Aggregated data provides information on worker satisfaction. It archives data from pre-hire, training and development, and ongoing performance assessments.

    Collecting and sorting this data has fallen to Human Resources, but technology empowers integration and evaluation of the data making them Information Leaders valued for discovering worker concerns and capabilities. The data that once determined the workers' tenure now shapes their work with 360° feedback capabilities.

2. Data has taken on a new role in defining an organisations' trustworthiness. The information builds trust that comes from transparency. This data supports and sustains the organisation's best business practices, ethics, and goodwill.

    With today's smarter customers, workers, and competitors, the data must satisfy their sense of completeness and clarity. Data-driven information survives deep due diligence and best practice scrutiny despite easy access to the internet.

3. Organisations that pass internal and external scrutiny build a shared sense of purpose directly and indirectly. When all stakeholders have access to valued information, all work and customer experience profits.

    Bias-free data offers a benchmark for the performance assessment of individual and organisational progress. The data is the means to align with value-added goals, measures readily apparent to the public on the internet, and social media reviews and comments.

4. Emerging technology applications and platforms have eased the work of organisations, workers, and customers. Workers enjoy work that challenges and ensures their accuracy. Educated machines like computer-assisted lathes correct errors, learn from experience, reduce labour, and provide quality outputs.

   Automation has enabled next-day delivery of purchases engaging and retaining customer experience and satisfaction. AI helps marketers put preferred products in front of shopping prospects and loyal customers.

5. Organisations can leverage their technology to increase their workers' autonomy. It puts decision-making information and tools in their hands and can train them as they work.

   Technology also enables customer autonomy and engagement by letting them choose size, colour, and delivery date and time. Customers can customise and personalise purchases thanks to interactive "dialogue" with the seller.

In these ways and more, technology helps organisations satisfy their customers and workers. Satisfaction is realised best when it is mutual and reciprocal, and technology drives this inter-relationship.

These are means that ease work and improve engagement. However, technology must also prepare organisations and their stakeholders to sense impending crises, recover from disaster, and reorganise after the disruption. The crucial information lies in the data available, so they must use it well. After all, even the best resources require best practices.

With structure, resilience, and frameworks in place, the "smartest" organisations have found opportunity in the changes forced upon them by the spread of COVID-19. They found the wherewithal to absorb the shocks and adapt their process and promise to the altered realities.

Such resilience is critical for organisations where international terrorism or systems of natural disasters regularly threaten them. They must have more reliable means and methodologies on hand to pivot, new and evolving ways to reduce impact and reshape their futures. COVID-19 was just one reminder that many executives have little immediate experience with such high-impact changes.

Challenges in the Future of Work

The transformation in the nature of work presents challenges to Executive Leadership because the transition means adjusting a legacy of coercive bureaucracy and top-down socialisation. Figure 9.1 summarises these leadership challenges:

THE LEADERSHIP SHIFT

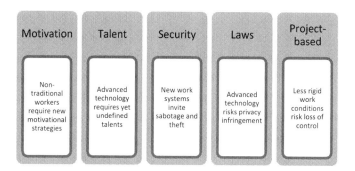

Figure 9.1: Leadership Challenges in the Future of Work

- **Motivation to Work:**

  Research showed a 17-point decrease in motivation for employees working remotely and surveyed between 2010 and 2015 (McGregor & Doshi, 2020). The researchers assumed that unhappiness increased during the COVID-19 pandemic lockdown. Consequently, the organisations planning to launch or grow their remote work units must learn to manage the motivation, alignment, and connectedness of those workers.

  It also means acculturating work associates to new relationships with machines, computers, and tasks that require cognitive resources, training, and talent. Much of future work will use more brain and less brawn. It will take leadership skills and talents to help associates move past perceived hurdles and embrace more sophisticated work.

- **Talent Shortage:**

  There is no shortage of people wanting and needing to work. However, new work requires skills and talents that require some development. Changes will need people to create and manage multiplying machines. A beverage bottling plant, for instance, may produce millions of products per week under the guidance and monitoring of just a few people. This "advance" has a substantial social impact, and schools have been slow to prepare students for this reality.

This disruption finds more people competing for the most menial jobs and the most envied jobs. Executive Leaders are not positioned or accountable for slowing or reversing this global transition. However, they must anticipate the impact of talent recruiting, placement, and retention on their future organisation. You will see, for example, organisations reaching afar to locate necessary leadership talent, which, in turn, diversifies the executive succession demographic.

- **Cyber Security:**

As organisations expand their reach, accelerate their technology, and increase their databases, they also increase their exposure. Even the smallest organisations participate in widespread communications. Their databases and information flow remain accessible to the threat of cybercrime.

Criminals hold corporations, hospitals, and municipalities hostage, demanding ransom before their captors release them. The world's largest organisations have seen their databases compromised with the theft of millions of identities. Even small organisations have found their customer data, proprietary information, and financial records stolen by inside or outside cybercriminals.

Executives will see these crimes continue and develop in sophistication. While they cannot be expected to police the threats, Executive Leaders must seek Trusted Advisors who can help manage the risk.

- **Digital Laws:**

  Citizens everywhere are concerned about their privacy. They object to real or perceived privacy threats as digitisation expands its scope and power.

  > *"Data privacy rights is one of the most urgent issues in contemporary digital policy. In the face of insurgent citizen activism and outcry, national governments are looking for options to address this problem - something difficult for many jurisdictions when they lack robust, responsive policy frameworks"* (Goggin, Vroman, et al., 2019).

  Establishing comprehensive standards on the use, provenance, governance, and transparency of individual and organisational data will prove difficult. Defining and framing policy, process, and penalty for widely diverse nation-states and their respective cultures and position on human rights has been challenging the highest global authorities. However, some regulation is inevitable. Organisation leaders must anticipate the impact on their respective practice and purpose.

- **Project-Based Work:**

  The Gig Economy is one sign of a global move to more project-based work. An emphasis on project-based work will change your view of organisational and operational hierarchies. It will integrate the linear logic of manufacturing processes with the agile and improvisational acuity of entrepreneurship.

The immediate task identifies the education, skill, and talent gaps among providers, employees, and executives. It strengthens functional work units with co-creative teams. Moreover, Executive Leaders need to model, engage, and enable a fluid and flexible mindset to stretch, reach, and affect real change.

Work often changes faster than the capabilities of workers. As technology accelerates and digitisation expands, education and preparation fall behind. The future presents a turning in the ability to order and forecast experience. Transformation requires resilience, and "resilience" means more than coping and responding to change. Such instincts only maintain the status quo, and the status quo is static and tactical.

New work and disbursed work demand strategic Invention and Innovation. For organisations to leverage strengths and deliver goals, they must understand, respect, and develop their potential for optimising digitisation. They must adopt and adapt technologies they can see, and they must understand the pros and cons of unseen technologies.

Imagining the future of work takes two paths. First, Executive Leaders expect labour to change as robotics, machine learning, and Artificial Intelligence influence work design. Second, the compounded effects of the recent COVID-19 pandemic and the emerging social context require Executive Leaders to think differently about the workplace, the processes it houses, and the talents necessary for sustaining growth.

The future of work presents such complex challenges. Threats and opportunities offer risks requiring courageous decision-making on the part of Executive Leaders. However, you cannot manage this alone. The future of work demands the integration of teams' skills and capabilities, including Trusted Advisors, if you want to prepare the organisation's readiness and resilience to pivot toward sustaining success.

Here's Your Takeaway

Whatever the future of work means for organisations, you must not lose connection with the customer experience. Advanced and accelerating technology affords new opportunities to optimise your customer experience journey.

However, change is partly necessary and partly discretionary. It falls to Executive Leaders to decide what investment and resources will make a difference in customer satisfaction, future growth, and talent management.

To improve decisions, you must remain current on information, devices, and execution, and this may require identifying the most Trusted Advisor on technology.

Chapter 10: Orchestrating Omnichannel Customer Experiences

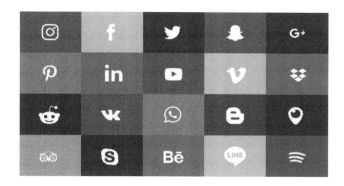

Here's What to Expect

- ✓ The challenges before an omnichannel customer experience
- ✓ Creating a "delighted" customer
- ✓ How to ensure a customer-centric experience

A new world exists where prospective customers can walk by a store and obtain real-time personalised offers or receive notifications. In some cases, customers can interact and suggest the price they are willing to pay to buy a product or service.

Virtual, augmented, and mixed realities enable customers to try before they buy in a digital world, so they do not have to leave the comfort of their home. To transform their customer experiences, organisations must dig deep into their customer journeys and proactively use technology like AI to extract real-time analytics, predict, personalise, and provide an authentic omnichannel experience. They must understand where their customers are struggling to complete journeys and be able to inject the right level of supportive guidance in real time.

The internet has changed the shopping experience. Customers have sacrificed those brick-and-mortar shopping experiences for online shopping. They have moved from a tactile experience to different decision-making processes where they explore the inputs, feedback, and reviews of others online.

Shoppers are not there to touch and try products physically. Today's customers turn to multiple digital platforms to comparison shop, read reviews, and watch demonstration videos. Organisations do well to make their product, image, and reputation available in as many ways as possible. They create a multi-sided virtual store using Chatbots, Smartphone apps, Social Media platforms, and other access tools.

In many settings, it appears to the customer that "the right hand does not know what the left hand is doing." The store's ordering process does not match the pricing online, or the Contact Centre Customer Service Representative does not know the product specifications. Omnichannel Customer Experiences improve such experiences with the strategic and functional integration of multiple customer interactions.

However, you might understand this better if you distinguish between Multiple Channel and Omnichannel customer experiences.

- **Multiple Channel** marketing optimises the brand's presence on known high traffic channels. They will secure their message on a website, in their blogs, on prominent social media, and so on. You might think of these as parallel vertical approaches.

- **Omnichannel** marketing sends a consistent message across all customer devices. Customers will access the product on smartphones, smart TVs, desktops, laptops, tablets, and any other device with internet access. You might think of this as a horizontal approach weaving images and messages across channels and devices.

According to a 2016 McKinsey study:

- "75% of online customers expect help within 5 minutes.

- 70% of app users prefer added functionality over 'look and feel' of the app.

- 61% of customers are more likely to buy from companies that deliver custom content.

- 75% of consumers have used comparison apps for consumer goods.

- 79% of consumers trust online requires as much as personal recommendations" (Duncan, Fanderl, Marchler, & Neher, 2016).

Organisations must present an Omnichannel Customer Experience. Their success depends on creating, launching, and sustaining a holistic approach to the customer's journey.

Here's My Story

A large retail organisation was upselling and cross-selling products to its customers without first understanding their requirements and behaviour. In the absence of a holistic view of its customer, the organisation was in constant sales mode, unaware the customer had open support tickets and overlooked issues.

Furthermore, in some cases, the offerings varied depending on the customer's channel (i.e., online versus in-store). Marketing campaigns were inconsistent and not addressed holistically because teams operated in silos.

Having identified the root cause of these issues, together with the executive leadership I orchestrated the delivery of a new omnichannel enterprise-wide architecture that addressed these marketing and customer experience inconsistencies.

With the core brand promise at the forefront, the key was to unite the various customer lifecycle departments and align sponsors to organisational strategy, key objectives, and metrics, including ownership of business case benefits.

They had built the organisation on the premise of always offering the next best action across all the customer-facing channels. Not only did this solution reduce the Average Handling Time (AHT) of contact centre inquiries and resolve operational inefficiencies, but it also helped the organisation realise over $200M in incremental sales.

The Customer Journey

According to a McKinsey Report, "*Customer journeys consist of a progression of touchpoints that together add up to the experience customers get when they interact with companies. Seeing the world as their customers do helps leading companies better organise and mobilise their employees around customer needs*" (Gammeri & Breschi, 2017). A clearer definition of "customer journey" suggests it represents "the customer's transition from never-a-customer to always-a-customer" (Ang & Buttle).

Various people picture different steps in the customer journey, and it helps if you can map the journey. It helps the leadership, management, rank-and-file associates, and customers see and understand its process and progress. It illustrates how each part of the organisation relates to that journey.

1. **Need:** Feeling a need to satisfy a want or need, customers look for input. Some customers actively pursue satisfaction while others are less active but alert to marketing messages they pick up from friends, co-workers, print and television ads, and now from Facebook, Twitter, and other social media.

2. **Fit:** Organisations build customer profiles over time. They should be alert to any customer interest, but they certainly should pursue that customer interest if it fits the marketing profile. For example, organisations can target social media users by age, race, gender, location, and more.

3. **Close:** Online sales close differently than in-person sales. In-person sales personalities and drive can affect a purchase.

Customers shopping online can always walk away, but they have only to click a button on any of their digital devices to secure immediate and free delivery. Online transactions remain impersonal.

4. **Return:** Organisations promote repeat sales actively. While online marketing may appear passive as it awaits customer initiatives, Omnichannel marketing will keep the brand and product or service fresh in the customer's mind while seeking after-service reviews.

5. **Fan:** Omnichannel customer approaches help buyers make your brand the "go-to" option. Customers resist changing suppliers and strongly recommend the brand to others by reviewing, ranking, and rating the brand.

Figure 10.1: Customer Journey Touchpoints

There was a time when people always bought the same car brand because their father and their father's father had always purchased that brand. If an organisation wants to earn that loyalty today, it must work harder, systematically, and strategically. Omnichannel marketing makes that customer journey a different experience, one that leads to profit for the organisation. It should use messages and images to develop awareness, shape opinion, coach consideration, and narrow the preferences that lead to purchases.

Mapping that customer journey identifies the touchpoints, each of those customer interactions where things can go right or wrong.

Challenges before the Omnichannel Customer Experience

"*At the heart of the challenge is the siloed nature of service delivery and the insular cultures, behaviors, processes, and policies that flourish inside the functional groups that companies rely on to design and deliver their services. In many cases, these groups are also the keepers of the touchpoints that shape and measure how the company's activities meet the customer's — say, an instore conversation with a sales rep, a visit to the company's website, or a query to the company's call center*" (Duncan, Fanderl, Marchler, & Neher, 2016).

When customers call the Customer Service Centre, they unwittingly enter a group with its own agenda in many businesses. The instinct is to protect the department's interests by blaming Shipping & Receiving or Sales. While these organisational "feuds" work themselves out, the customer's journey stops in its tracks. Some organisations exacerbate the problem by physically locating operations attached to each touchpoint in distant worksites.

On the other hand, the digitisation enabling Omnichannel Marketing experiences can cut through those silos putting everything necessary in front of the customer.

- **Slow to invest:**

Executive support is critical. *"One of the challenges holding back omnichannel efforts is lackluster commitment on the part of leadership"* (Hennick, 2019). Retail analyst Sucharita Kodali writes that several senior executives interviewed in 2018 *"still don't prioritize digital channels enough and focus instead on their core businesses and historic capabilities"* (qt. in Hennick, 2019).

- **Failure to meet customer needs:**

The reviews of customer satisfaction are ubiquitous across the internet. Dissatisfied customers quickly report their unhappiness on rankings with Google, Yelp, Glassdoor, and Facebook. Too many executives dismiss such dissatisfaction as a sunk cost, just something that comes with being in business.

- **Good service is no longer enough:**

Customer satisfaction has no universal metric. Customers may like the fast delivery but dislike the fit or the colour but not the fabric. They come up with a unique set of disappointments. However, Omnichannel tactics can remove, deter, or resolve those complainants at numerous touchpoints.

- **Lack of customer-centricity:**

Without the personal interaction of brick-and-mortar sales, online customers can miss the human touch of social connection. However, you can personalise Omnichannel customer experiences with customer-centricity embedded in their culture and core values.

- **Failure to follow up:**

  It is quite possible that customers are more satisfied with a follow-up call than they are with the purchase itself. The follow-up shows concern and respect, but it also provides an opportunity to ensure a happy customer becomes an advocate.

Creating the Delighted Customer

Most organisations aim to meet the customer's expectations. Too many organisations are satisfied with that when they should seek to exceed customer wants. The most successful organisations work to create delighted customers.

Inc.com published principles of customer delight, saying, "*Delighting customers is about more than just meeting their needs in the moment. It's about building authentic relationships that stand the test of time*" (Ehrlichman, 2014).

1. **Respond quickly.**

   Fast response is crucial. Any delay allows the competition to intervene in what would have been an excellent opportunity to listen.

2. **Listen well.**

   Every email, phone call, social media review holds value for Executive Leaders. Entrepreneurs and Lean Startups are well-positioned to profit from customer feedback as they develop and test new products.

3. **Satisfy need (not want).**

Customer insight and input are invaluable. However, the organisation has multiple obligations to various stakeholders, so it must pursue achievable and useful deliverables.

4. Surprise them.

Customers want to be valued. They can be fickle and will pivot to the competitor who offers something they did not expect. They can be high maintenance, and Omnichannel Marketing can assume that care and comfort. Customers are *satisfied* when they get what they expected; customers are *delighted* when they get something more.

5. Personalise contact.

It does not take much to create a lasting relationship if you can give customers a contact person. You humanise the experience if customers have a name and number they can call for help. For example, some manufacturers enclose a phone number to reach them before the customer considers returning their product. They are confident they can help you over the phone.

6. Give them a break.

Organisations should build authentic relationships judiciously. You can implement regular contacts with customers without smothering them with calls or emails. Some customers complain about finding their shopping interests appearing on other sites. It seems to violate their privacy to see ads for products they considered on one website showing up repeatedly on others.

7. **Empower flexibility.**

Influential executives must empower customer contacts to respond with some flexibility. Firm standard policies support a functioning department; however, telling a customer that "This is the company policy" or "It's the way we do things" will not delight the customer.

8. **Maintain transparency.**

Customers are interested in how and when you will fix their problems. They want to know what steps you are taking to satisfy their concerns. Provide information on the process you are following, and the transparency and accountability will build authentic and lasting relationships.

Speedy response and active listening encourage innovation from the outside, inputs that lower prices and costs. One expert says,

> "*in traditional hierarchical bureaucracies, with multiple vertical layers of authority and many different departments and divisions, work jams are occurring all over the organization on a daily basis; typically, no one notices or does anything about them. Work sits waiting in queues. Approvals hold things up. Customers try to get answers and wait for responses*" (Denning, 2011).

However, customer-centric organisations enable, encourage, and empower agile and often improvisational customer response. The ability to remedy customer situations with speed and clarity becomes more critical when it operates across omnichannel platforms. Neither the customer nor the organisation can avoid the consequences of dissatisfaction.

How to Get There

Executive Leaders must take the lead in moving their operations to an omnichannel basis. Perhaps, the most local of mom-and-pop retail stores can avoid the inevitable. However, any organisation with an internet presence should appreciate and embrace this future of marketing through customer service.

Those executives will need help in realising Omnichannel effectiveness, but they should understand the importance of *delighted* customers. They will need professional advice, the outside talent capable of meeting and exceeding their expectations with a complex but customised infrastructure and execution.

Customer-centric organisations are winners. They delight the customer at every touchpoint. However, because each customer shops and buys from a different context, they favour seamless interactions across all the channels made possible by digitisation.

So, leaders benefit from our advice on market-leading strategic cloud technology, increased customer delight, and customised customer ecosystems.

Here's Your Takeaway

This chapter has reviewed multichannel and omnichannel approaches to customer satisfaction. Executive Leaders must distinguish Multichannel from Omnichannel technology and how they affect customer experience. The business you promote and the audience market you wish to target should draw you into deciding on the best-suited approach for reaching your goals.

In most organisations, the tools and strategies involved are too complex for existing internal functions. So, Executive Leaders must know enough about optimisation to work with outside Trusted Advisors about:

- How omnichannel strategies affect the customer experience,
- Identifying and creating a "delighted" customer, and
- Structuring a customer-centric interface and using data to test, continuously learn and innovate.

Chapter 11: Engaging Stakeholders and Managing Relationships

Here's What to Expect

- ✓ Define and distinguish shareholder and stakeholder
- ✓ Address the challenges to stakeholder relationships
- ✓ Recognise emerging disruptive trends
- ✓ Reimagine the future of work and workplace

Executive Leaders must ensure business outcomes are clear and understood by internal teams and stakeholders in this unpredictable world. Organisations with Executive Leaders who are ready, willing, and able to improve their leadership in managing relationships and stakeholders have significant business advantages.

Organisations with robust stakeholder and relationship management ensure their internal teams are:

- Learning and improving continuously
- Collaborating and self-organising, accepting ownership and accountability
- Experimenting and adapting
- Humble and bold.

Here's My Story

The senior leadership team of a large media organisation had not invested time in understanding the job functions and responsibilities of their peers and key stakeholders. Requests for action, reports and information were not understood and as a result were seen as a waste of effort, despite being a key reporting mechanism for the board. The root cause of poor stakeholder engagement is a culture that is content with the status quo. With a lack of external trusted advice and coaching, the organisation had spiralled into a world of inefficiency and waste. It was focused on performing tasks out of routine rather than reimaging the future and responding to change.

The framework established helped the team explore communication, connectivity, and stakeholder management in a transparent manner. It provided thought leadership on individual engagement, the rise of automation and the importance of agility with a constant feedback loop to ensure continuous improvement. It was an eye opener into the operations of the different business units and provided an open environment to collaborate, optimise and improve productivity. Executive Leaders with in-depth understanding of their respective teams will have a competitive advantage because they will bring out the best in their employees and drive 'best in class' productivity and organisational performance.

Stakeholders invest in an organisation and hope to share in its profits. That definition has long been limited to those who make a financial investment in the organisation—the banks, stockholders, venture capitalists, and others who provide the capital that allow the organisation to open its doors and continue its operations.

However, contemporary organisations also respect their executives, managers, employees, vendors, and customers as stakeholders who make various critical contributions to the organisation's success. The broadened scope includes a new emphasis on supply chains, consultants, and customers as vital assets.

Just about anyone touching the organisation, its products, or its services has a vested interest in how the organisation performs. The Return of Interest (ROI) has morphed into something more significant and often less tangible than a financial return. Nonetheless, financial shareholders represent an interest that must be honoured.

Shareholders Defined

"Shareholders" are people, businesses, or institutions that own equity in a for-profit organisation. They hold a piece of paper (a share) representing a share in the organisation's profit (and loss). These shares also represent the shareholder's risk in the organisation's realising its plan and potential.

Those investors also stand to lose money when the organisation's value declines. Such losses can trigger a series of events in which shareholders sell off their shares to avoid further loss. Other investors, watching that volatility in the markets where stocks are bought, sold, and traded, will continue the decline by selling their shares. Others, of course, will see an opportunity to buy while the shares' value has lowered.

The organisation agrees to reward that shareholder's risk with additional shares, increased share valuation, or dividends. When large organisations offer shares for investment by the public, it is considered "publicly traded" and will raise significant capital with that offering. The influx of funds helps the organisation grow, innovate, and compete.

The organisation may buy back these shares in the future to secure its ownership and reduce its obligations to the shareholders. However, it may also repeat the offering process to raise additional funds in the future.

Small organisations may attract the investment of lenders who are repaid by contract. Moreover, the small organisation that intends to remain small may depend on the "sweat equity" of family or first phase employees and partners. These investors expect equity compensation for their proportionate effort in beginning the organisation and establishing its path.

These stakeholders may have complicated relationships with the organisation—some secured by law and compliance oversight, and others formed and influenced by perception. Shareholders with extensive stock holdings have a voice in the organisation's decision-making. They may press the organisation to increase its performance or to optimise its community interests. They may voice their concerns about the organisation's profit decline or public perception of its political stance. In any case, the organisation must form and sustain favourable relationships with the shareholders.

Stakeholders Defined

Many others have a direct and indirect investment in the organisation's success.

- Supply chains depend on vendors and providers with a calculated interest in the organisation. The organisation is their customer, so they must understand its operation and its material needs to serve its customers.

- Maturing executives invest brains and brawn in growing and sustaining the organisation. Some organisations offer shares as compensation incentives for their talent and commitment.

- Senior and junior managers, supervisors, and rank and file employees throughout the organisation's hierarchy secure their positions and career paths by investing their talents and efforts to high performance in and across their functional silos.

- Customer consumers have strengthened their power and influence with their purchasing power multiplied thanks to social media and omnichannel marketing.

- Consultants grow in influence, needing organisations to succeed as a reflection of their counsel.

Executive Leaders sit at the nexus of all these forces. They hear all the voices, juggle all their concerns, and drive the organisation's future through these often-conflicting interests.

> "*Openness of markets, freeing up capital flow and globalization of production have created an interdependent world in the post-industrial era of today*" (Kimiagari, Keivanpour, Mohiuddin, & Van Horne, 2013).

Competing for investment in this world means "*value-based management and long-term value creation require the consideration of all stakeholders in the strategic decision-making process*" (Kimiagari, Keivanpour, Mohiuddin, & Van Horne, 2013).

Milton Friedman, the brilliant economist of the mid-20th century espoused a *Shareholder Theory* which claimed the "*only and sole purpose of business is to increase profits and value returned to shareholders (owners of the company)*" (Shareholder Theory). He taught that senior executives and hired managers

> "*are obliged to serve the interests of owners and make money for them, without particular regard to the welfare of society or employees. Managers act and decide only according to law without particular interest on ethical or cultural factors*" (Shareholder Theory).

However, others would come to criticise this approach as too narrow, counterproductive, and wrongly focused. They feared the emphasis on profits would lead to short-term results at the expense of the organisation's future, manipulating processes and reports, and unethical (or illegal) behaviours.

The equally renowned and respected R. Edward Freeman noted, "*We are in need of new concepts, new 'conceptual filing systems,' which reorient our way of looking at the world to encompass present and future changes*" (Freeman, 2010).

Freeman recognised a complex universe of stakeholders who interact directly or indirectly with organisational action, inaction, practice, and behaviour.

He lists the stakeholders shown in Figure 11.1:

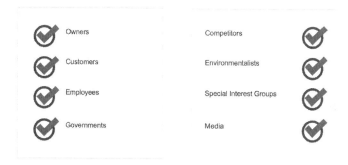

Figure 11.1: R. Edward Freeman Checklist

The *Stakeholder Theory*, then, holds the

> "*central task in this process is to manage and integrate the relationships and interests of shareholders, employees, customers, suppliers, communities and other groups in a way that ensures the long-term success of the firm. A stakeholder approach emphasises active management of the business environment, relationships, and the promotion of shared interests*" (Freeman & McVea, 2001).

These forces have made stakeholders of themselves. While organisations may not be affected by these forces equally, they no longer function independently of these influencers. It falls to leaders to acknowledge and resolve the challenges presented by the multiple stakeholders.

Challenges to Stakeholder Relationships

Senior Executive Leaders are expected to build relationships with their organisation's stakeholders. They routinely budget time and expense in financing events with their Board of Directors, for example. Some expect their Sales Department to wine and dine customers. Most will sponsor quarterly or annual social events for employees. However, the challenges presented by stakeholders require engaging them and keeping them engaged.

It makes good sense to establish collaborative relationships. Too many people misunderstand the idea of collaboration. They bring people together, put subject matters on the table, and toss around some ideas. However, collaboration calls for much more than this brainstorming.

True collaboration pulls together diverse people with varied experiences who are valued for their insights. Brainstorming may be a tactic that collaborators use, but it is not the essence. Collaboration requires the exchange of ideas, tools, methods, strategies, and more. When shared, argued, and refined among willing and engaged partisans, they produce solutions to things that challenge the organisation.

THE LEADERSHIP SHIFT

Many organisations fail to optimise the opportunities presented by engaged collaboration. Executives might profit from the inputs of employees and middle managers because they have shown respect for the contributors who demonstrate the following challenges:

1. Time and truth are tiring.

Building and sustaining stakeholder relationships is time-intensive. It carves out a large part of the executives' life and energy. Moreover, the stakeholders, having their special interests at heart, do not present an entire picture of the challenges posed.

Recommendation: Executive Leaders must identify the priorities relevant to those who speak for the stakeholder group. You must clarify why you are interested in their challenge and align their interests, processes, and objectives with the organisation's affirmed values. In short, stakeholders must feel your interest is focused and genuine rather than general.

For instance, the Sales Manager who treats the staff to pizza parties or an occasional golf round may please the team. Still, the social events do not engage the employees in innovation and agile approaches that further the department goals.

2. Stakeholders will shift shape.

Stakeholders change in personality and interests. They join up and grow with you, or they lose interest and fall out. It takes effort to sustain their loyalty.

Recommendation: Executive Leaders must prioritise the stakeholder relationship. Executives may come from many specialised backgrounds; naturally, their first interest pursues their unique talent—whether it is in finance, law, operations, marketing, or other disciplines.

However, they must adjust their thinking to give these relationships priority. They should delegate tasks in their specific discipline and focus on stakeholders as people—as individuals and as groups—who hold their organisation's future in hand. This increases the importance and value of reciprocal respect and communication. Orders from the top down in a coercive bureaucracy prove counterproductive as they prevent the formation of a psychologically safe environment where collaboration thrives and delivers.

3. Too much seems invested in too little.

Engagement can seem exhaustive when projects are small- or short-termed. Holding meetings, following agendas, courting members, these all take time. Sometimes, that time and effort do not appear to equal the weight of the outcome.

Recommendation: Organisations can overwork an issue. It takes some experience to balance the effort and results. There can be too much data, too many participants, too many objectives, and so on. Executives need metrics that master these loose ends.

However, Executive Leaders should keep stakeholder engagement a high priority. They must monitor performance indices to keep them aligned with producing and maintaining stakeholder engagement. Moreover, they must understand that stakeholder "satisfaction" differs from the "engagement" that integrates the stakeholders' interests with measured outcomes.

4. Engaging the unseen is a new problem.

All stakeholders have presence and value even when they are not seen and present. The suppliers and consumers may reside continents away. Many employees may work remotely. Even senior officers may live and work in countries far removed from the home office. Keeping them engaged and involved can be a challenge.

Recommendation: The internet has given virtual stakeholders a louder voice. The inability to meet one-on-one presents a real problem because people are social animals. Without personal contact, it is hard to read the relationship. Working through meeting platforms offers some contact but little connection. Engagement is more problematic when meetings lack the emotional connection afforded by in-person meetings.

So, you must make the most of the time you have. You can learn to master the technology, so it does not contribute to the distance. You might balance the group remote chats with personal and individual calls. You should prepare these virtual meetings with more emphasis on the personal and less on the data and slide presentations. It helps engagement when you can ask after someone's spouse or child, when you know their names and jobs, and when you can relay remarks by a happy customer.

5. **Good relationships are circular.**

Productive relationships do not follow straight lines. They need much more than a "give and take." Relationships Involve more than transactions. They should be dynamic based on an organic framework that grows as it metabolises inputs.

Recommendation: Executive Leaders view stakeholder relationships as systems. The participants should not work independently of the organisation's common interests and values because the flow and rhythm to the relationships resist linear description. You cannot draw quality relationships on the horizontal, moving from left to right. Engagement is fluid and expansive. It supports, informs, and fuels success rather than push and drive.

Trending Disruption

Disruption has ruled the first quarter of the 21st-century. Terroristic attacks occur frequently. Local and global politics are increasingly divisive. Volatility dominates economies. A viral pandemic has killed globally and brought populations to their knees.

Organisations originate, manage, and resolve disruption everywhere. From a less lofty view, their leaders must look to stakeholder engagement as a levelling force. Keeping stakeholders engaged trumps keeping them involved, so you need to identify and employ the necessary drivers. (Enright, McElrath, & Taylor, 2016).

Enright, McElrath, and Taylor identified five trends affecting organisations into their respective futures:

- "*Trend 1: Communication, Connectivity, and Hyper-Transparency*
- *Trend 2: Individual Empowerment and the Rise of the Middle Class*
- *Trend 3: The Demographic Shift and the Automation of Work*
- *Trend 4: The Primacy of Climate Change and Water Resources*
- *Trend 5: Supply Chain Oversight Ramps Up*" (Enright, McElrath, & Taylor, 2016, p. 2)

However, their work focused on global organisations while I see these drivers at work on organisations of all types, sizes, and purposes.

Trend 1: Communication, Connectivity, and Hyper-Transparency

The organisation's communication, connectivity, and transparency drive stakeholder engagement, and these are all responsibilities of the executives. Where employee communications were once left to Human Resources and customer communications left to Customer Service, Executive Leaders must assume accountability for the crafting and delivering of engaging communications.

Messages and methods must link multiple interests persuading those in Human Resources responsible for recruiting, hiring, and developing employees to commit to customer service and engage in a customer-centric culture. Leaders must leverage the technology that disrupts the organisation's interests. *"Business leaders can no longer control the timing, content, or interpretation of the information that is disclosed about their companies"* (Enright, McElrath, & Taylor, 2016, p. 6) on multiple platforms with global reach.

Leadership must accept this new reality. Executive Leaders must make it positive by stepping up their communication quality and quantity to forestall criticism and profit.

Trend 2: Individual Empowerment and the Rise of the Middle Class

Concepts of equity have changed. Where workers once expected wages for the work completed, they have joined a universal expectation of a revised social contract that supports them more broadly.

The spread of democracy, socialism, and mixed economies have altered the worker's sense of fairness, social justice, and benefit. Their relationship has moved from a servant mindset to one where they have a voice deserving respect and response. Moreover, the internet has extended the reach of materialism and consumerism, driving envy and redefining what is meant by "workers' rights" and "middle class."

> *"It is also likely that as expectations around business responsibilities shift, the sector will need to place a greater focus on the sustainability of the local*

environment, societal challenges, and the equitable sharing among stakeholders of the value created by development" (Enright, McElrath, & Taylor, 2016, p. 7).

While this will drive an organisation to political, social, and environmental activism, the Executive Leaders can harness the power for positive outcomes that serve stakeholders and the organisation's goals.

Trend 3: The Demographic Shift and the Automation of Work

This century has already seen significant shifts in population. Poverty and war have forced emigration that challenges the cultural standards of established societies. These arrivals fill jobs disdained by native populations, significantly altering the culture's sense of itself. Such shifts rarely occur without the resentment that leads to violence.

Religious, political, and economic forces drive the multiplying diaspora. People cross borders seeking many objectives and filling low-pay, low-skill jobs. However, their movement coincides with advances in work automation, widening the gap between the immigrant and established workers.

"*To prepare for emerging demands, businesses should begin to assess their evolving roles, market demands, and stakeholder expectations as early as possible*" (Enright, McElrath, & Taylor, 2016, p. 8) because those expectations will come at organisations from increasingly numerous directions in increasingly diverse languages.

Trend 4: The Primacy of Climate Change and Water Resources

Climate change and the availability of resources are no longer academic issues alone. Supply chains have proven weak and vulnerable, and more organisations compete over the same resources and raw material. Famine happens here while volcanoes erupt there. However, they are not isolated incidents in far-off places. In a world where organisations have global aspirations, whatever happens on the other side of the globe affects stakeholders on this side of the world.

Your organisation is not independent of another organisation, no matter how radically different they may seem. This interdependency requires organisations to *"engage with communities in a substantive way, creating a form of partnership by providing communities with a voice in business decision-making"* (Enright, McElrath, & Taylor, 2016, p. 9). In time, only community partnerships respecting natural resources and climate will ensure resilience and survivorship.

Trend 5: Supply Chain Oversight Ramps Up

The trade wars and pandemics dominating recent history have taught many lessons about supply chains. Nation-states found themselves desperate for personal protective equipment for medical practitioners. Nation-state leaders leveraged supply chain failures into international political issues. The supply chains would, in turn, shift their performance to states with favourable payment patterns.

That vulnerability marked the fragility of these relationships. Supply chains have depended on recordkeeping and paperwork, multiplying copies for monitoring, filing, and auditing. Any supply chain, then, involves scores of touchpoints subject to error or failure. When you multiply these risks times the delivery logistics, the several competitors, and the changing needs of the organisations and its customers, you see the size of the threat.

Any supply chain has a start (supplier) and finish (customer); however, thinking of supply chains as horizontal progressions is reductionist. The functioning supply chain has multiple influencers from Purchasing Departments, Inventory Supervisors, Manufacturers, Shipping & Handling Departments, and more. When your supply chain also crosses borders, it moves through governance, compliance, and other monitors. Even the purchase of office supplies has become a global event.

Organisations will find *"A structured approach to identifying, managing, and mitigating supply chain risk will not entirely protect companies from reputational risk"* (Enright, McElrath, & Taylor, 2016, p. 10). However, the consequences of insecure supply chains during the spread of transglobal infections like COVID-19, SAARs, and Ebola have taught more significant lessons.

Reimagining the Future

Talk of "a new normal" is a regressive and sentimental wish if it favours the status quo over accepting, adopting, and adapting to a new future. Organisations need evolving resilience and adaptivity to emerging internal and external challenges.

A key strength of leaders and executives is their ability to anticipate. They are no better at predicting the future than anyone else, but they are sensitive to what is coming towards them. Much of this strength arises from strong relationships where Executive Leaders:

- *Value* relationships with stakeholders as resources that strengthen and grow the organisation.

- *Share* information and experiences that prepare them to collaborate and co-create solutions to problems not yet seen.

- *See* and test the potential and profitability of new products, services, and markets.

- *Listen* to employees and customers whose partnerships empower organisation futures, and

- *Keep* their Boards and Investors fully informed on best standards and practices.

Executives must do more than push an organisation forward. They must reimagine their future as a living organisation, an organic flow that responds to the local and distant ecosystems that make a difference. They are expected to be consistent, but consistency is not linear. *Consistency* requires more than *constancy*; it refers to the internal character making solid decisions under pressure—to design change rather than submit and to know and reward all their stakeholders.

Here's Your Takeaway

Executive Leaders have unique relationships with Shareholders. Shareholders hold the leaders accountable for achieving a Return on their Investment. However, Executive Leaders of contemporary organisations have found that addressing all Stakeholders' concerns serves to drive the growth performance that rewards Shareholders' interests.

Having established strong relationships, the Executive Leaders will respect the organisation's governance providing the decision-making information they need or mandate. There are challenges before Executive Leaders and their mandate to build and sustain stakeholder relationships. They are challenged to reimagine the future of work and the workplace in the face of emerging disruptions and trends in a volatile climate.

Chapter 12: Corporate Governance and Managing Information Flow

Here's What to Expect

- ✓ Understanding data as an asset
- ✓ Differentiate between data and information
- ✓ Governance depends on information flow
- ✓ Follow the information flow
- ✓ Execute a strategic framework
- ✓ Map the information flow
- ✓ Secure executive sponsorship
- ✓ Assess the use of a PMO
- ✓ Ensure continuity of governance

It takes multiple teams and subject matter advisors to resolve the most challenging customer experience problems. Cross-functional partnerships and trust become crucial to secure the scalable ability to tackle these challenges. Organisations with leading governance and information flow ensure successful transformations through:

- A culture of trust promoting honesty and transparency,
- Constant feedback loops encouraging difficult conversations holding each other accountable, and
- Employee empathy for their colleagues' positions, inputs, and points of view.

All organisations require a structure consistent with Governance and Executive Management. It needs an infrastructure to support its decision-making. Internal and external stakeholders need assurance that responsibilities, accountabilities, and compliance principles are clear, established, and functioning effectively and efficiently.

- Governance: "*The systems and processes concerned with ensuring the overall direction, effectiveness, supervision and accountability of an organization*" (Governance, Management, and ..., 2009).
- Management: "*The act of directing and controlling a group of people for the purpose of coordinating and harmonizing the group toward accomplishing a goal beyond the scope of individual effort*" (Governance, Management and ..., 2009).

However, this understanding is dated. The emphasis on people underestimates how management has expanded to include accountability for finances, technology, competition, innovation, and much more. In doing so, the thread tying everything together is Information Flow.

Here's My Story

Despite the many benefits of our digital era, there are also several unintended consequences that have emerged. One of these is the problem of information overload. The leadership team of a Fortune 500 organisation spent their time focusing on superficial details, including how a meeting pack should be presented, rather than providing support and guidance on the challenges faced. Lack of transparency and trust was preventing real optimal information flow to aid accurate decision making. Some leaders were concerned with irrelevant presentation protocols than ensuring there was engagement from their peers, having the right conversations or ensuring the team was focused on solving the right challenges. Ultimately, they were not connected to the real issues and therefore unable to make the right decisions.

THE LEADERSHIP SHIFT

With the right leadership coaching and corporate governance advice, the focus shifted to the key themes and issues that resonated with peers. This was a catalyst for positive change and helped drive trust and confidence amongst the executive leadership team. It was imperative that fundamental challenges in the organisation were surfaced at the executive level without fear. A strategic execution framework was set up to help navigate the complex issues and provide opportunities for collaboration, alignment and prioritisation to orchestrate strategic outcomes. This process was indispensable in providing clarity to the business strategy and objectives. By assisting in the development of key outcomes, we were able to capture and measure success of the strategy and provide a benchmark for success.

Governance Depends on Information Flow

Organisational integrity and transparency require optimal Information Flow. If organisations are to build trust and drive stakeholders to reach stretch targets and higher values, they need information-rich data.

A disconnect here can present significant problems. For example, the International Transparency Organisation has scored the integrity of Australia's business, political, and organisation integrity at 77 on its scale of 100 or ranked 12 of 180 countries measured (Australia, 2019).

The ranking has caused significant concerns across the nation. *"Australia is among 21 nations where perceived corruption has worsened 'significantly' over the past eight years"* (Knaus, 2020). *"The [Australian] government has faced persistent calls to introduce a strong, well-resourced national integrity commission. Draft legislation for its proposed model – criticised as weak by many integrity experts – still has not eventuated, despite promises it would be ready by the end of last year [2019]"* (Knaus, 2020).

The highest-ranked nations include Denmark and New Zealand. Their smaller size indicates some of the Australian problem has to do with the size and complexity of its organisational environment, mixed economy, and political standards.

Nonetheless, this makes headlines that damage the reputation and appeal of organisations with questionable and vulnerable integrity. The necessary "Information Integrity" requires accuracy and consistency if Executive Leaders must depend on their trustworthiness. Systems, processes, and people behaviours must comply and align to ensure a total picture.

The Information Age has seen exponential growth in the volume of data. It continues to assess quality and material efficiency. However, information has taken on its own life. Its collection, farming, harvesting, and storage create a dynamic more extensive than earlier years' accounting systems.

- The abundance of data creates *a new dynamic.* Despite its binary architecture, the sheer volume of data holds an organic dynamic, driving research, prototyping, testing, and comparative results.
- The data contains *autonomous information,* independent of the originators, managers, and users. However, they can effectively influence the information's bias.
- The data supports information as evidence. However, finding and phrasing the patterns in the data *invites subjective myopia.* Integrity requires systems that limit or prevent subjective inputs and end users.
- Even firm data and autonomous analysis *risk errors and misrepresentation* when converted to text to communicate to internal and external stakeholders.

Most important is understanding that information is a corporate asset. It is material and fuel for organisational progress. As with other assets, the organisation consumes the information, which has the potential for exhaustion and waste. The organisation metabolises the data converting its "chemistry" and "energy" into new outcomes. Finally, the organisation distributes information designed to fulfil end user expectations. This flow-through is its great utilitarian strength, but each touchpoint risks failure or abuse.

The quality of the information enhances executive leader decision-making. The accuracy makes it reliable and their decisions trustworthy. Decisions based on ill-prepared and poorly verified data risk loss of productivity, investment, reputation, and competitive position.

Organisations with holistic approaches to management, strategy, and performance succeed as a function of best practices in information management. They respect information flow as an organic process instead of a pass-through process, an overall monitoring flow strategy, and triggering continuous self-improvement along the way.

Following the Information Flow

Unfortunately, fundamental problems often fail to reach the surface. All organisations are

> "*made up of constructs in which people can have access to information and speak to each other. Modelling information flow for organisations is a challenging task that enables analysts and managers to better understand how to: organise and coordinate processes, eliminate redundant information flows and processes, minimise the duplication of information and manage the sharing of intra- and inter-organisational information*" (Durugboa, Tiwarib, & Alcock, 2013).

THE LEADERSHIP SHIFT

Any organisation is a complex system of systems. One of those systems is the organisation's Information Flow. An organisation will metabolise incoming *data* in the form of facts and figures. It searches for *informative* patterns and context in the data. Processing the data and information produces *knowledge* with positive, negative, or neutral values.

An organisation's hierarchy brings data up to the senior decision makers. They are expected to use the knowledge they have drawn to add value to the organisation. This is a product that must be tracked, archived, and inventoried. However, that Information Flow is never a straight line.

- **Vertical** dissemination follows the information from the highest organisational level through the executive charged with each functional silo. The data also flows up through the same functions. Metrics focus on the flow's efficiency and expediency.

- **Horizontal** dissemination tracks the information across functional silos. Leaders of different and disparate functions share values in the information as it is parcelled out. As the data moves across functional silos, the functions refine and refocus it for their purposes.

- **Relational** dissemination occurs when information is consciously or unconsciously communicated to colleagues and peers. However, the relationships may be more subtle as when information is shared with golf partners, family, friends, or other unauthorised figures. This flow can add organisational politics to the mix.

Each of these communication lines may be focused and constrained or unfocused and loose. It is crucial, then, to control the information flow if the organisation expects to retain the value of its information and knowledge.

- **Centralised** delivery assigns the dissemination of information to a specific person or department. This achieves a consistent communication style enabling more control and accuracy. However, it may appear conservative, judgemental, and unresponsive.

- **Decentralised** delivery sees each functional department, division, or region produce the wisdom of its knowledge. This controls the quality and quantity of information fresh from "the horse's mouth." However, there is no consistency when departments compete because there is no incentive to develop cross-functional relationships.

Strategic Execution Framework

Our work often discovers a damaging disconnect or misalignment among strategy, structure, process, and technology capability. Information loses its value when it is not well understood, prioritised, and utilised.

Executive Leaders must embrace technology as a complete structural and strategic partner. The function has long surpassed its helpdesk utility. Once limited to servicing the organisation's network, hardware, and software needs, technology now plays a more central role in finance, marketing, sales, human resources, engineering, research, and the remaining organisational functions.

Information is a crucial integrating part of organisational purpose. Figure 12.1 lists the key elements of real and perceived corporate integrity. With quality information, Executive Leaders will:

- frame and model core values,

- encourage trust with psychologically safe work environments,

- engage members in work and purpose of value to them,

- promote personal and functional honesty and complete transparency,

- attract talents to support, implement, and achieve transformation, and

- ensure compliance with a rigorous set of standards.

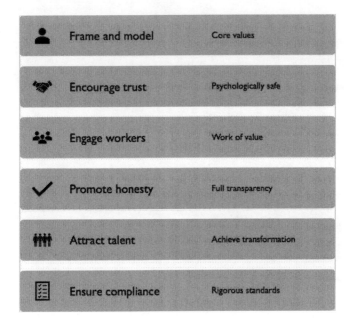

Figure 12.1: Keys to Organisational Integrity

No longer limited to a vertical focus, technology must integrate all organisational purposes, plans, and processes. So, organisations need technology champions at the highest level, expert orchestrators who know how to value and manage Information Flow.

Simply put, you do not want to be the next organisation to fold because you have not adapted to changing conditions. Some 79 percent of organisations surveyed by KPMG in 2017 said, "*advanced technology was a 'must have' in the next 5 years*" (Broderick & Witte, 2017).

However, many organisations find themselves invested in technology network structures and systems.

> *"Many years of customer focussed innovation has resulted in hundreds of products or services. Each of these has a range of features, and each of those features drives process variants, all supported by a combination of legacy technologies and human operations"* (Vega, 2020).

However, KPMG's survey of 200 Australian chief executives would find digital transformation the top concern keeping them up at night. The results ranked the concern above perennial issues like the global political and economic environment, regulation and regulatory environment, and innovation and disruption.

The survey asked executives to focus on these questions:

1. *"Do you have top down, CEO-led sponsorship for the transformation?*

2. *Is your entire business aligned with these goals, and have you updated incentive systems to align?*

3. *Have you had more than one previous program that was unsuccessful?*

4. *Do you have lots of other competing priorities?*

5. *Is your legacy environment so complex that you can't understand it?*

6.   *The biggest question, however, comes from facing squarely up to the epic challenge of complete digital transformation and asking: do we have it in us?"* (Varga, 2020, p. 9).

Answering these questions honestly and thoroughly still does not address whether you have the tools, strategies, and capability to suit your organisation's specific Information Technology needs.

A 2020 KPMG survey identified digital transformation among the top concerns of Australian business leaders. They want to increase customer satisfaction, operations efficiency, and financial reporting. However, they now see organisations accelerating IT use to widen marketing reach, brand performance, and retain talent.

As a McKinsey report puts it,

> *"The COVID-19 pandemic has heightened the need for companies to adopt digital business models—and only cloud platforms can provide the agility, scalability, and innovation required for this transition"* (Arora, Catlin, Forrest, Kaplan, & Vinter, 2020).

The executive level of any organisation cannot fully grasp the scope of advanced technology. It is not their responsibility. However, they must sponsor transformation if the organisation is to move forward. Few people have the knowledge or experience in execution, but any transition requires a culture and mindset ready for change.

Senior executives must identify and support the orchestrators, those who know how to improve and manage the information flow. They will build the strategic framework to execute information capabilities.

There are steps you can take to effect and execute the transformation. Executive Leaders must:

1. Set the strategic direction for the role of Information Technology.

2. Assess and reconfigure the organisation's structure for supporting a strategy of transformation, including the role of "self-directing" teams.

3. Review the processes and technology capability for supporting the strategy.

4. Reimagine the organisation's relationship with Information Technology as a partnership rather than a functional silo.

5. Secure the advice of and execution by a Trusted Advisor.

Without this route to discovery, executives are not up to the transition effort. In the survey language, they do not have it in them.

- **Clarify the strategy.**

  Any strategy must target the problem you want to solve. A successful digital transformation will integrate technology, processes, and the people whom the strategy impacts. Executive Leaders and technology partners must align their thought and action with organisational purpose.

  Executives concerned about what their experience brings to this challenge should focus on the problem needing a solution rather than the technology itself. After all, technology will continue to change. If you focus on the technology and not on the problems, you will always end up chasing technology without any concrete solutions to the organisation's original challenges like:

1. Increasing and improving self-service for customers.

2. Creating richer and more innovative customer experiences.

3. Introducing robotics and automation to increase efficiency; and more.

Despite the ubiquitous chatter about advanced technology and artificial intelligence, these are tools—not solutions. Without a strategy, functions will overbuy, underbuy, and double buy tools, not solutions.

- **Practice a healthy ratio of information implementation and consumption.**

A healthy technology strategy balances implementation and consumption. Users consume information with some constancy. Assuming for the sake of illustration that an organisation follows a workweek with five days of eight hours, stakeholders consume information throughout those 40 hours, albeit with different intensity.

However, organisations exist beyond the 40-hour workweek. Information and interaction continue their flow, and customers access your systems 24/7. Global organisations feed information consumers without end.

That continuing consumption reduces the time available for implementing a digital transformation strategy. So, any digital information strategy must have a timeframe for information consumption per day/per week. While the organisation may delegate consumption management, the technology managers and champions must spend two to three times those hours initiating, planning, and executing strategy.

It is good to stay current on technology changes, but consuming too much information can lead to decisions based on what is new and available rather than on what you need to meet specific strategic goals. When information is only one Google search away from learning what you want about technology, it can easily overwhelm you, shifting your attention from business goals before making critical strategic decisions.

Senior executives must distinguish tech hype from its reality. Failure to use technology smartly and adequately only leads to a failed digital transformation strategy.

- **Create productive and promising teams to affect digital transformation.**

The successful execution of any digital transformation strategy depends on the people and talent involved. The best teams include people driven by a sense of clear purpose, those people who have demonstrated a collaborative mindset with an approachable and open nature.

Team members' capability to understand and execute transformation takes precedence over budgeting allegedly cutting-edge digital tools. Prominent organisations repeatedly fail to meet their digital strategy goals because of poor leadership, weak executive sponsorship, ineffective governance, project complexities, and more.

You must first determine if the organisation is structured for change, agile enough to implement and deliver a digital transformation strategy. Some 46 percent of global talent leaders rank finding a robust and capable team as a significant obstacle (Abbot, Batty, & Bevegni, 2016).

Complex and challenging digital transformation requires a team that fully understands collaboration and has demonstrated the innovative openness to doing things differently. Executive Leaders are tasked with selecting their teams, identifying their leaders, and leveraging their talents to make change happen.

You can build strong, capable teams when you look for the following:

1. **Sense of Clear Purpose**

    The most effective teams include people who can get to the core reason for digital transformation quickly. They prioritise strategic goals over technology tools. They recognise and value the purpose and benefits of transformation and have the talent to communicate the vision of improved organisation-wide benefits, a strengthened competitive edge, and a more productive place to work.

2. **Collaborative Mindset**

Real and effective transformation does not occur in isolation. Executive Leaders are responsible for securing a broad and deep commitment to collaboration as a strategic tactic and culture. They must ensure an enabling workplace environment where every voice is heard and leveraged.

Most employees want the organisation to succeed. All employees of any organisation want to be part of a bigger picture. They seek and enjoy the respect shown for their talent and contribution. Well-framed challenges and changes energise and engage their work.

The failure to leverage their potential only leads to the organisation's inability to optimise digital transformation efforts.

3. **Approachable and Open Nature**

Collaboration does not work unless team members and leaders are approachable and open. Change and transformation can foster conflict and emotional response.

People follow those who are approachable and open. They work best with those who care about the organisation's future and those who listen and hear their voices. If team leaders fail to show interest and accessibility, people will walk away to someone who cares about their views.

The best teams are led and peopled by employees who combine these traits. However, you will find that staffing these teams, structuring their behaviour, and integrating their purpose and outcomes require trusted outside advisors' talent and experience.

Map the Information Flow

Figure 12.2 illustrates a "best practices" Execution Strategy Framework to keep alignment at the centre.

Stuart's Strategic Management Framework

| Effective Strategy Management | Prioritisation | Alignment | Executive Governance | Orchestration |

Execution 12.2: Execution Strategy Framework

From some perspectives, the information should track upwards. However, direction and placement do not present a strategic concern. Organisation transformation—whether launched with purpose from within or forced by external conditions—calls for a framework that prioritises, aligns, governs, and orchestrates the change.

Remembering that strategy means little without execution, the framework must enable the execution of priority short-term outcomes while strategising and orchestrating long-term goals for the future. The prudent use of time and resources offers a competitive edge over other organisations focused on solving short-term problems without seeing more ample opportunities.

Future-focused leaders may understand and tolerate uncertainty. However, it can be challenging to see a brighter future in times of crisis. An Execution Strategy Framework is a key to resilience.

It will help you regain perspective, solve current critical problems, and map future success opportunities.

Prioritise Key Tasks

Evaluate what your business is doing right now. Identify what needs to change and make it a top priority for the organisation. This means removing departmental KPIs in favour of organisational ones.

Boost Employee Morale & Verify Shared View of Strategy

Make employees aware that you value their wellbeing. Help them understand the benefits of a strategic management framework and their role in the orchestration of its delivery.

Ensure Effective & Efficient Executive Governance

The key to Executive Governance is to ensure your framework adapts to a constantly changing environment and fosters a sponsorship coalition enabling transparent communication throughout the organisation.

Orchestrate Delivery & Prepare for Future Upturn

With essential tasks prioritised, employees cared for, and all leadership levels aligned, you have more time and energy to strategise for your organisation's future.

These steps, taken together, produce an effective strategic management framework.

Nevertheless, Information Flow informs and enables each phase of the strategy. You need quality data to prioritise the necessary tasks. You want the data-based information to align employee interests with organisation purpose, the resilient and responsive information that fosters emotional connectedness, and the future-forward information to visualise results-based performance amid and through critical periods of transformation.

The Need for Executive Sponsorship

Information Flow depends mainly on the connectivity and performance of Information Technology, but IT delivery taxes budgets. It also requires specialised knowledge that top-level executives often do not share. However, value-added IT projects advance organisation performance as well as provide information that confirms organisational integrity.

Designing and launching projects require executive sponsorship, the financial and functional backing that gets things done. Crawford and Brett (2001) offered this list of responsibilities for the executive sponsor in descending order of importance in Figure 12.3 (Cooke-Davies, Crawford, et al., 2006):

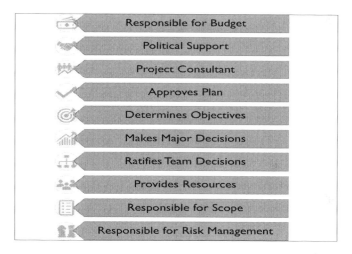

Figure 12.3: Responsibilities for Executive Sponsor
(in descending order of importance)

Executive Leaders run successful organisations, advised, and authorised by Boards of Directors and shareholders to:

1. **Empower executives to sponsor.** Projects require the backing and underpinning of officers with the appropriate authority to make decisions, leverage needs, and manage the project's politics.

2. **Possess personal and political influence.** The executive sponsor needs direct access to the final authority. The sponsor must have direct relationships with key figures in the

organisational hierarchy, players necessary to project completion.

3. **Able to integrate and align.** An Executive Leader sponsor must design and forge links between the respective project and the organisation. Project managers need the broader vision and organisational awareness of that sponsor.

4. **Willing to press the project through.** Multiple needs will pull at Executive Leaders. However, Sponsors will nurture and promote their sponsored projects to expedite their completion, ensure their necessary resources, and prioritise peers' and colleagues' support.

5. **Motivate and incentivise project management and teams.** Team members value the manifest support and commitment of an Executive Sponsor. It provides confidence in their project's importance and adds value to their stress in reaching the targeted date.

6. **Remain responsive and accessible.** Priority projects depend on the ability to reach their sponsors. Executive Sponsors are quick to provide a nurturing response without sacrificing their broader responsibilities. With experience, the sponsor and sponsored will build trusting partnerships that honour their respective needs.

7. **Communicate honestly and thoroughly.** Communication skills enable leadership and build trust. The sponsor relationship requires superior formal and informal

communication. It achieves expectations and aspirations using positive and constructive communication.

8. **Partner with peers and players.** Few projects are solitary. Every aspect of IT, for example, touches other functions in the organisation. It takes talent, position, and decisiveness to energise others' interests, useful or necessary to the project's realisation.

9. **Pushback with understanding.** Project Team Managers want and seek pushback from their Executive Sponsors. They are looking for approval, yes, but they want support from someone who knows what and why they are working on the project. If they are to collaborate fully, the sponsor must be involved in the collaboration. The sponsor must not only demonstrate patience but also provide constructive guidance. Good Executive Sponsors are accomplished coaches.

10. **Decisive and focused in the face of complexity.** Executive Sponsors expect to *own* the projects underway. They expect, respect, and pursue clarity. They will repeatedly rephrase and parse a situation until they have eliminated all ambiguity. They want the process and the results to be "an easy sell" if they are to take it on.

The Executive Sponsorship portfolio still needs management. Transformation happens at many levels. The personnel (including executives) will change occasionally. Needs, budget, tools, and team members will change. Context, environment, and political conditions will vary. Organisations function in a volatile world.

Change risks inconsistency, lack of coordination, and conflicts of interest. Leadership heads its way through such challenges. The Executive Leader's skill set, experience, and emotional maturity should withstand fragmentation and strengthen aligned values.

Using a PMO

Information flow circulates through an organisation's systems of systems. Information feeds all the organisation's functions from concept to delivery. However, it also enables governance and standards. In a competitive world, it nurtures morals, ethics, and compliance lest greed compromise organisational purpose. Information shapes a conscience where there is none.

- Prudent Executive Leaders may consider forming or outsourcing a Project Management Office (PMO). A PMO *"sets, maintains and ensures standards for project management across that organization. They're the keepers of best practices, project status and direction — all in one spot"* (Miller, 2017). The PMO may be a creative presence, an idea bank with little effective authority. It might notice needs, propose solutions, and design practices to enable results on an ad hoc basis.

- It may be built as an administrative office. It will provide oversight, monitor the project management progress, prepare reports, and offer support when requested.

Ideally, a PMO will be formally structured and empowered to:

- set policy and enforce practice,

- allocate budgets and resources,

- control schedules and staffing,

- "police" key performance indicators (KPIs), and

- prepare reports, including continuous improvement.

This formally structured PMO is a department reporting to the Chief Executive Officer and providing vital services and information to the executive team and its Board of Directors. It must avoid focusing too much on its "little picture" of things and obsessing on KPIs to exclude other elements. Still, it can add value to the organisation and its executive experience.

A functioning PMO will help executives transition to new positions and transition from one organisation to another. It ensures continuity and allows Executive Leaders to fulfil their responsibilities by taking a critical task off their desks. However, there is no one best format for a PMO; organisations should avoid templates. Effective Executive Leaders will look for consultants who can analyse and customise a PMO for their requirements.

A Continuity of Governance

This chapter examined the value added when an organisation acts "rightly." However, history has shown that humans and their organisations wrestle with deciding on and doing what is right. Understandings of things good and bad vary greatly, and lest an organisation be unsure about matters of conscience, it needs guidance, principles, procedures, and oversight.

In the presence of doubt about decision-making, ethics, morals, and laws provide resilient frameworks. Local, regional, and global legislatures have created layers of obligations primarily out of necessity. Organisations should operate legally, comply with legal mandates, and report as required to compliance agencies. Nonetheless, you cannot underestimate the complexity required by law.

An organisation needs a principled Board of Directors—independent of conflicts of interest—to accept final accountability, provide direction, and make information-based decisions of lasting importance to the organisation and its stakeholders.

Good governance requires the design and implementation of best practices throughout the organisation, practices conceived and managed to reduce risks of real and perceived damage to people, places, and purpose.

Executive Leaders must identify and profile all stakeholders to build the relationships necessary for consensus-building and customer-centric decisions. Throughout these processes, the organisation must gather, archive, and report information on its performance with accessible transparency. This transparency must detail and assign accountability for all decisions affecting stakeholders.

The continuing COVID-19 effects of 2020 will alter the governance mandates. Emerging factors will assign new mandates on workplace health and safety. Additional legislation will mandate more reporting and compliance. As formal and informal governance increases and finds its new best practices, Executive Leaders will face new and expanded accountabilities.

Finally, good governance expects organisations to demonstrate behaviours that ensure internal strength and continuity as well as external perceptions. Both markets and stakeholders prize reputation, and without consistent and admirable governance, the business and loyalty they generate will suffer.

Here's Your Takeaway

Organisations have complex, multilayered obligations to fulfil, multiple demands for compliance and proof of good governance. Executive Leaders are directly accountable to private, public, and governmental agencies. This includes numerous complicated reports which a good Information Flow feeds.

Organisations also have complex operational dynamics requiring extensive data resources and multiple technologies. These systems require decisions on purchasing, implementation, and maintenance. Information hardware and software must align with business goals.

Executive Leaders must understand their liability for best practice accountability and create and monitor a system that ensures transparency and compliance.

Section 4

Chapter 13: Building an Organisational Culture of Employee Engagement

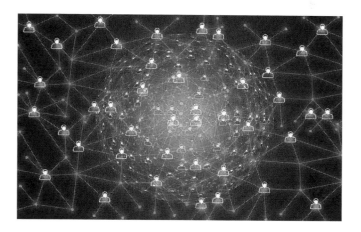

Here's What to Expect

- ✓ Understand the nature of culture
- ✓ The modes of organisational culture
- ✓ The signs of healthy and unhealthy cultures
- ✓ Add value to the context of organisational culture
- ✓ Keep things aligned

Every organisation has a culture. It may be the one you want—or not, but a culture will take shape. The culture can be purposeful, positive, and productive. It can be divisive and disruptive. It can lie somewhere in between. Employee Engagement remains a key metric in defining the culture.

People must work differently if organisations are to achieve cultural transformation. They must adopt and adapt to advancing technology, evolving processes, and innovative tools to maximise ROI. Such a paradigm shift can only work with people focused on the change process. Organisations—expecting to survive and disrupt markets beneficially in this new but volatile world—must continuously revisit and adjust their culture to ensure Employee Engagement leads every executive leader's objectives.

> " *While there is universal agreement that (1) it exists, and (2) that it plays a crucial role in shaping behavior in organizations, there is little consensus on what organizational culture actually is, never mind how it influences behavior and whether it is something leaders can change*" (Watkins, 2013).

Nonetheless, Executive Leaders must deal with the culture in which they find themselves. As leaders, they remain accountable for the organisation's outcomes, and culture is the context in which they operate. They must identify the cultural elements that add value and those that do not, so they can build one that only adds value.

This chapter tries to develop a fuller understanding of organisational culture and examine the role of Employee Engagement in the formation and sustainability of culture.

Here's My Story

A large global and Fortune 500 financial organisation was struggling with cultural issues causing division between business units. It struggled with employee motivation, loss of Intellectual Property (IP), and heightened compliance risk. Moreover, there were multiple unsuccessful attempts at transitioning and integrating new clients onto their platform, including restructuring and significant technology and process changes.

I was engaged in orchestrating transitions and coaching leadership teams to create centres of excellence. On initial assessment there were conflicting priorities and a lack of alignment on the key goals and objectives, resulting in employee disgruntlement. There was no shared vision or a clear sense of purpose.

It was a must to create a great environment that fostered emotional connectedness by demonstrating the right behaviours so that employees felt empowered. A culture of transparency and trust was vital to ensure positive employee behaviour and ultimately high performing teams. It would provide employees with a platform to support company initiatives and recognition of good work. The success built a sense of community that allowed employees to feel part of something bigger than their job description. I worked with the leadership teams to align business and IT, including employee motivational triggers to ensure healthy collaboration and dialogue that ultimately led to having high performing teams.

Understand the nature of culture

A starting definition holds, "*Culture is the characteristics and knowledge of a particular group of people, encompassing language, religion, cuisine, social habits, music and arts*" (Zimmerman, 2017). According to The Centre for Advanced Research on Language Acquisition, culture is the "*shared patterns of behaviours and interactions, cognitive constructs and understanding that are learned by socialization. Thus, it can be seen as the growth of a group identity fostered by social patterns unique to the group*" (Zimmerman, 2017).

The Leadership Shift seeks to tie culture to organisations, their strategies, and their results. Here are eight aspects of organisational culture:

1. It is "just the way we do things here."

You see culture in the behaviour of organisations and the people that populate the organisations. That is, it is observable (signs, symbols, slogans, and so on).

2. It is what you pay for.

Compensation will drive culture. Incentives will purchase ambition, achievement, and allegiance. Rewards and recognition create and sustain loyalty. However, inequities and bias in compensation will weaken morale and culture.

3. It is carried forward in stories.

Stories of the organisation's achievements will continue the culture forward. Organisations should develop and reward storytellers for helping others fit in and belong.

4. **It does not exist independently.**

An organisation's culture belongs to a system of systems. Unique as an organisation thinks it is, the culture still reflects other social norms, frameworks, and expectations. For instance, North Americans are used to a five-day, 40-hour workweek, whereas Europeans expect prolonged vacations. These behaviours are replicated in workplace value systems.

As one system functions interdependently on other systems, an organisation has multiple overlapping subcultures. For instance, the Logistics group may have its own characteristics. While they may clash with Sales & Marketing's expectations, at the core, they espouse the same aspirations. It is also true that large global organisations may build on mergers and acquisitions of other systems with their specific cultural stamps.

5. **It is shared complexly.**

Culture is a social concept, one that requires full buy-in by its members. It is a conscious or unconscious collaboration on beliefs, goals, and objectives. This commonality helps reduce disagreement, divisiveness, and dissent when everyone is "on the same page," culturally speaking.

6. **It comes from social connection.**

Humans draw together instinctively. They find an advantage in numbers when in "fight or flight" situations. They form communities out of self-interest and find they must integrate with others to sustain the organisation. Since well before written history, humans have grouped to feed, clothe, and shelter themselves.

However, once they discovered the advantages of staying still and participating in trade, they formed more complex organisations. To manage the complexity, organisations defined and embraced behaviours that define them. They introduced policies and procedures to keep members in line, which risks building a restraining and constrictive organisation.

7. It keeps things healthy.

Culture protects the organisation and its members. The stronger the culture, the more likely it is to survive challenges. It becomes a resilient core, a totem to which members cling when the organisation, its principles and purpose are attacked. Conversely, it can blind leaders and members to valuable forces outside its walls.

8. It is organic.

In time, the organisation's culture becomes embedded in its DNA. It grows and matures, and it suffers and collapses with time, abuse, and lack of attention. Leaders more than members are responsible for enabling and empowering the positive and monitoring and managing the negative. Ideally, you will want to develop an evolving culture with continuity, scalability, and sustainability.

The Modes of Organisational Culture

Banking on your understanding that you know culture through its observable behaviours, you can discern different modes of operation:

- **Command and Control:**

  An organisation that values policy and procedure more than fluidity and flexibility is a Command-and-Control Culture. It enforces systems that deny dynamism in favour of hierarchy. It incentivises allegiance and compliance. It promotes stability and predictability. Command and Control Cultures dominate government bureaucracies, although you will find them in research institutions, banking, and other fields.

- **Compete and Adapt:**

  Free markets and mixed markets favour organisations with stability and standards. However, they prefer organisations with cultures that "*have an external orientation and they value differentiation over integration*" (Tharp, 2009). That is, the culture feels competitive. Globalisation has rewarded Competitive Cultures because they focus on relationships. These organisations understand that they depend on supply chains, customer loyalty, and efficient productivity.

- **Diverse and Collaborative:**

  Collaborative Cultures value flexibility, agility, resilience, and responsiveness. They seek integration instead of regimentation. They are more likely to pursue a matrix than a ladder, coherence rather than order, and teamwork over individual efforts. Entrepreneurial efforts can optimise this cultural approach, positioned, as they are, to build an infrastructure to continue the culture through future growth. However, it remains difficult for an established hierarchical structure to change its culture.

- **Creative and Agile:**

  A culture can encourage creativity by enabling and empowering ad hoc responsiveness to challenges. Such organisations continue with a satisfactory procedural framework, but they encourage autonomy and flexibility. In a competitive economy, organisations must look outside for cues to pivot and take another direction. They must adapt continuously and rapidly, so agility and flexibility are highly valued. Even established organisations must pursue innovation in products and services.

  However, most organisations combine different modes. They are hybrids. For example, the first stage entrepreneurial startups tend towards a horizontal approach wherein everyone brings passion and energy to multiple tasks. As organisations expand, they move towards silos identified by function (accounting, marketing, and so on). Still, driving a dominant mode is crucial to avoiding confusion and misdirection among stakeholders.

Executives are obliged to direct, model, and develop the organisation's culture. Their most critical tool is their ability to observe and listen. They must watch and study behaviours and listen to the voices of both the dominant culture and its subcultures. Unions form, for instance, where voices are neither heard nor acknowledged.

Signs of a Healthy Organisational Culture

Healthy organisations have manifest cultures that attract and retain talent and customers. Some signs of their health include:

- **Robust Branding:**

    Public images, brands, mission statements, and the like project multiple messages. They offer a shared sense of purpose that holds people together, connects them with their leadership, and binds them to the communities served. People inside and outside the organisation respond positively to images of people engaged in the organisation's work and the work they produce.

- **Employee Retention:**

    While stable organisations have a regular rate of employee turnover, healthier organisations attract applications and retain talent. Executives lead great companies "*by sparking deeper emotional connections with colleagues – by aligning your values, collaborating, cocreating a positive future, giving respect, and focusing on achievement*" (Carter, 2010). People stay with organisations where they feel needed, wanted, and loved. When mutual respect is the transactional currency within an organisation, talent thrives and makes a difference.

- **Trust-based:**

  Executive Leaders have a healthy organisation culture if *"they trust their employees enough to let them get the work done where and when they choose"* (Ryan, 2018). Employees do not expect license to work at will, but they engage better in collaborative and challenging work. They prefer projects and initiatives to job description task lists.

- **Good Air:**

  A walkthrough at a healthy organisation sees employees engaged in crafts, teams, and self-directed work. There is an air of camaraderie, a psychologically positive environment where fear and sanctions are not usual or formative. A psychologically positive environment enables "flow"—

  > *"a state in which people are so involved in an activity that nothing else seems to matter; the experience is so enjoyable that people will continue to do it even at great cost, for the sheer sake of doing it"* (Csikszentmihalyi, 1991).

- **Good Work:**

  A healthy culture focuses on quality work. Metrics focus on work fulfilment and effectiveness rather than quantity and efficiency. In a healthy culture, executives are close enough to the floor to respect, recognise, and reward good work and the talent that enables and empowers it. Executives stress how good work contributes to the organisation's goals. With this weight on the positive, the organisational culture avoids the negative.

- **Balanced Wellbeing:**

Members of a healthy culture see little difference between their work-self and their real-self (Ryan, 2018). Their work world and real-world experience become seamless. Instead of avoiding or leaving work behind, members remain aware of and involved in both aspects of their lives. They identify with the work as part of their total experience, something with values larger than sustenance.

- **Community-conscious:**

Organisations are only one segment of a social and environmental ecosystem. Outsiders and would-be members look for organisations involved in their local, regional, and global communities. First-stage organisations may sponsor local youth sports. Growth organisations may volunteer work in local emergencies. Large organisations may offer philanthropic support for significant causes. Moreover, organisations feel increasing responsibility for environmental concerns.

- **Equitable Compensation:**

Organisations must pay members in accordance with the law. The lowest-performing cultures offer the lowest compliant pay. Organisations perform better if their compensation and benefits structure compete in the labour market. However, the most positive organisations step up and into future-forward compensation structures that allow members to actualise their aspirations. It will enable them to grow and stretch as individuals and social beings.

- **Customer-centric:**

  Organisations that build and sustain customer relationships attract talented people who want to contribute to customer satisfaction. They appreciate a role in making customers healthy, wealthy, and wise. They see customers as teammates whose feedback they value. They seek to join organisations focused on customer satisfaction, loyalty, and growth.

- **Positive Reviews:**

  When unemployment is high and jobs scarce, people will make concessions to secure sustenance for themselves and their families. If the organisational culture is positive, those employees will work hard to see the organisation prosper. However, when unemployment is low, workers at every skill level have more choices, and they will research the many online resources reporting on organisations and their cultures. Executive Leaders can ensure positive reviews by listening and responding close to the source of employee experiences.

A healthy organisational culture can delegate many of the tasks sustaining its continuity. However, the Executive Leaders must lead the culture. They must maintain a holistic approach and model the desired behaviours.

Signs of an Unhealthy Organisational Culture

Gallup reports, "*Companies with highly engaged workforces outperform their peers by 147% in earnings per share*" (The Engaged Workplace, 2020). However, "*87% of employees worldwide are not engaged at work*" (The Engaged Workplace, 2020). The results of Gallup surveys on engagement have dominated management news for some time.

You should understand these surveys are self-reported. That is, influence the results. Such surveys help but also present some problems; for example, the concepts questioned and reported vary from culture to culture. Moreover, for employees surveyed at work in low-income economies, engagement is not a primary concern.

Nonetheless, an organisational culture with strong employee engagement is more likely to succeed, whereas "*low engagement results in burnout, higher levels of turnover, and counterproductive work behaviors such as bullying, harassment, and fraud*" (Chamorro-Premuzic, Garaad, & Elzinga, 2018).

- **Discouraged Workers:**

  Workers become discouraged for many reasons. They do not get the respect they expect. Workers have always provided effort in exchange for compensation. This was quite clear when most labour was piecework. However, the understanding of *effort* and *compensation* has evolved.

  "Effort" now requires collaboration, agility, and commitment. "Compensation" now includes pay, benefits, and social offsets. Workers discourage quickly if their effort is not respected, integrated, and delivered.

They are discouraged when their employee-employer contract fails in comparison with their peers' position. Organisations that fail to enable and empower worker autonomy also frustrate workers who could make a difference. Finally, "discouraged workers" include those who have given up, have surrendered their ambitions in the face of broad and deep unemployment conditions.

- **Withdrawn Workers:**

  Disengagement at any organisational level appears in the members' reluctance to contribute, participate, and communicate. They may nod approval or disapproval, but they are not involved.

  They take a virtual leave of absence. Dissatisfied workers hold back mentally and physically. They resist intelligence sharing and slow their productivity. They exploit passive/aggressive behaviours, and silence becomes a weapon. This withdrawal represents a change in behaviour and routine, affecting team and organisational goals negatively.

- **Concerted Action:**

  In some environments, concerted adverse action will attract disengaged workers. Union organisers sense this vulnerability and will launch concerted activities against the employer. While organisations can work effectively with unions, they can avoid additional union restrictions on their autonomy.

Concerted action can take other forms. Disengaged employees may damage productivity, consciously or unconsciously. They may form a subculture with unhappy and frustrated peers; together, they can influence and undermine.

Even worse, they will sabotage the process and outcomes. They hurt the organisation with their resistance, reluctance, and outright theft of their assets and intellectual property.

- **Poor Management:**

  Executive Leaders must look to the organisation's management for causes and solutions to employee disengagement. Coercive hierarchical environments drive compliance with policies and procedures. This approach restricts and stiffens. It discourages co-creative collaboration, agile response, ad hoc resolution, and hearty engagement in organisational goals.

  Micromanagement strikes emotionally mature workers as minimalist and reductive. Micromanagement builds on prohibition and sanctions only to narrow and negate vision, mission, and purpose. Boxed in by tight oversight, workers disengage from the work.

  Conversely, Executive Leaders must recruit, equip, and develop leads, team leaders, supervisors, managers, and high-potential leadership. They must do so with engagement in mind. Disengaged managers will not enable engaged workers.

- **Cynical Climate:**

  You have a problem when employee cynicism and negativity thrive in the organisation. Engaged employees are likable, involved, and constructive. Disengaged workers are resentful, distant, and disruptive. You can feel this around the water cooler or in the break room.

  Influential Executive Leaders must walk around routinely if they are to sense the vibe empowering a cynical culture. They should listen to what is being said and try not to react to the person. They need to accept the voice as feedback, deserving integration and resolution. These leaders must also "walk" around the virtual workplace triggered by the 2020 COVID-19 impact.

  Cynicism and frustration are tangible. You can measure, analyse, and resolve the causes and conditions, allowing the negative attitudes to continue.

Executive Leaders will observe, address, and resolve the context in which employee disengagement thrives and survives. They must monitor their organisations to discern what needs fixing. If you are transitioning to a new organisation or expanding your own, you should structure the operation and climate to secure and sustain employee engagement.

All stakeholders have voices. Shareholders, executives, managers, or rank-and-file stakeholders want to be heard. The voice may damage the facility or the community; it may take the form of concerted action. Hopefully, the voice will reach the executive level without malice. However, this only happens in a climate where you listen and listen well.

The Context of Organisational Engagement

Among your crucial accountabilities is the retention of talent. Employee turnover and the loss of talent is a cost that organisations cannot bear for long. The financial cost of recruiting and replacement is daunting, and the cultural loss of key talent is exhausting. So, Executive Leaders must prepare a culture that nurtures and sustains talent, one that can adapt to the necessary and inevitable turnover that will occur.

The environment must ensure meaningfulness, safety, and availability:

- *"Meaningfulness is the degree to which workers invest themselves into their role performances and experience a return on that investment, such as feeling valued by the employer."*

- *"Safety implies that the employee feels comfortable to show the self without negatively impacting the self-image, status, or career."*

- *Availability is the worker's belief that he or she has the physical, emotional, and cognitive resources to engage the self in work"* (Kittredge, 2010).

It must face a multidimensional, multilayered, and multifaceted challenge with no simple framework. They must structure and maintain a culture of engagement despite nuanced challenges:

- **Socio-psychological Antecedents:**

As individuals, employees have some level of emotional intelligence. Few employees share the same level at the exact moment. However,

> "*as employees feel like the organization shares their personal vision for their work and feel positive about and supported by the organization for whom they work, they will likely be more engaged in their role as organizational members*" (Mahon, Taylor, & Boyatzis, 2004).

- **Perceived Organisational Support:**

Stakeholders have always responded positively where executives provide tangible support. However, a study of responses by New Zealand dairy workers found,

> "*Intrinsic reward satisfaction was relevant to both job involvement and affective commitment, while extrinsic satisfaction also played a role in the prediction of affective commitment. The finding that intrinsic satisfaction contributed more than extrinsic satisfaction suggests that interventions based on job enrichment (for instance, increasing variety, challenge, and decision latitude) may have a more beneficial influence, on job involvement especially, than increasing material rewards, such as pay and fringe benefits*" (O'Driscoll & Randall, 1999).

- **Emotional Intelligence:**

A study of Australian police officers identified a strong correlation between Emotional Intelligence (EI) and job satisfaction, commitment, and wellbeing. It proceeded from a definition taken from John D. Mayer and Peter Salovey:

> "*the ability to perceive accurately, appraise, and express emotion; the ability to access and/or generate feelings when they facilitate thought; the ability to understand emotion and emotional knowledge; and the ability to regulate emotions to promote emotional and intellectual growth*" (Brunetto, Teo, Shacklock, et al., 2012).

- **Emotional Connectedness:**

  An environment of psychological safety encourages emotional connectedness (EC) among employees, between management and employees, and between organisation members and the institution's structure and goals.

  > "*Emotional Connectedness – high personal connectedness and high organizational connectedness – drives discretionary effort, more creativity, positivity and more desire to collaborate*" (Cohn, 2018).

  Louis Carter, the founder of *Best Practice Institute*, reports:

  > "*Love of workplace or Most Loved Workplace (MLW) is the intersection of intense feelings toward aspects of a company, perception of how your company feels about you, and attitudes toward respect and treatment of employees. Our study proves that intense amorous feelings for the workplace are a greater predictor of organizational outcomes such as organizational*

commitment and perceived willingness to produce more for the company" (Cohn, 2018).

Great leaders create great environments, even in such complex contexts. Their stakeholders all share specific characteristics, and the organisation excels when these cultural keys are in sync. (These characteristics are based on those found in Volo, 2014).

- **Celebration:**

From the top down, management must celebrate achievements—big and small. Rewards and recognition should be frequent and loud. There is a need for fun, humour, gifts, and toasts.

- **Connectedness:**

Connection occurs in cultures that stress shared values and purpose. However, Executive Leaders must model this connection, reiterating its importance as an ideal and practical step towards success. You do not unite people by requiring them to comply; you attract them by modelling exemplary behaviour.

- **Collaboration:**

Employees engage through collaborative work and fun. It requires reciprocal and mutual interchange and integration. However, collaboration requires structure, so employees and managers can positively connect and develop common interests. Executives would do well to understand collaboration is like a conversation; it cannot be a one-way effort.

- **Contribution:**

  A customer-centric organisation helps members understand their role in the market and with the people who shop there. It has a sense of giving back to the community and the other systems in its universe. This sense of giving back encourages members to provide more and better impacts.

- **Creativity:**

  Innovation and Co-collaboration only occur in enabling environments. Continuous Improvement just prospers where permitted. Productivity only surpasses the norm where autonomy and agility are valued.

Keeping Things Aligned

Executive Leaders are expected to align workers and work. They develop high-level performance teams aligned with the organisation's future. They are accountable for retaining the talent necessary to accomplish the organisation's goals, and talent retention depends on their direction, optimism, and consistent commitment to the organisation's values.

Circumstantially, this means creating and sustaining strategic efforts. Organisation leaders must:

- **Respect the organisation's members need a life/work balance.**

Of course, Executive Leaders do not hold hands or resolve individual problems. However, they should immerse themselves in compensation packages and the nature of work. They should understand that talented team members do not produce when stressed, so empathy must flow from the top down.

- **Develop high-performing teams.**

Executive Leaders must identify and develop inspiring team leaders and talent that creates energy and enthusiasm. Leaders empower and enable collaboration. They develop and achieve stretch goals with trust in their purpose-driven focus.

- **Strengthen team alignment.**

Executives should live and breathe their organisation's mission. Every stakeholder must share a vision of what and why the organisation does what it does. They must know and respect the audience they serve and the values they bring to the customer experience.

- **Study the organisation's rhythm of work.**

Executive Leaders should feel the organisation's rhythm. That is, they should appreciate its natural routine as a factor in the context for its innovative and creative reach for stretch goals.

- **Provide tools and resources.**

Organisational leaders must remove barriers to achievement and provide the technology to achieve success aligned with organisational purpose.

- **Make IT a strategic partner.**

  Many organisations continue to treat the Information Technology department as a help desk—rather than a strategic partner. Technology is so much a part of operations, so effective executives should leverage its potential value to align work with purpose inside and outside the organisation.

- **Elevate Human Resources.**

  Legacy institutions relegate Human Resources to an administrative and prophylactic role. HR must set and enforce behaviours that comply with various governing agencies. However, prudent organisations have recognised HR's value as a partner in defining, identifying, and developing talent aligned with the organisation's goals.

Executive Leaders have accountability for a healthy corporate culture. Healthy cultures follow healthy, centred, consistent, purpose-driven leaders. People look to leadership for information, motivation, and inspiration. Executive Leaders must take an active role in making this happen.

Senior executives cannot do this on their own. They need advice and assistance, coaching and development, and support and experience. However, they should regularly survey the elements expected of a healthy organisation. An organisational health check can be lengthy and complicated, but it helps to keep it simple.

For example, you might survey the following as clues to areas needing focus in management:

1. How strong is employee motivation?

2. Do employment and workplace conditions promote work and engagement?

3. Do employees know what the organisation expects of them?

4. Are you confident you have what you need to manage employees and their work?

5. Is the organisation recruiting the talent needed to succeed?

6. How well do you understand the difference between responsibility and accountability?

7. Have you been able to reduce worker turnover?

8. How well are your teams engaged in their work?

9. Do the people you oversee trust you?

10. How would your employees rate your performance?

There are other questions, of course, and you can conduct surveys of employee views at the same time. With assistance, you can integrate and analyse the scoring to identify the pain points needing help.

Here's Your Takeaway

This chapter examined the complex context in which people work. Their engagement in their workflow, an atmosphere of positive psychology, a climate of emotional connectedness, and a tradition of aligned purpose—these accountabilities belong to Executive Leaders.

During the entrepreneurial phase, you can inspire these values, but there are steps that you must manage if you are transforming into an environment weak in these organisational virtues.

However, culture creation and management may be too much for a single Executive Leader. Executives turn to consultants for direction and strategy. They seek support in unexpected situations and where their efforts have failed.

Just as there is no prototypical organisation, there is no one solution. There is no template for strategic alignment, so you may want consultants experienced in customizing strategic responses. For instance, you might use an outside consultant to create and conduct employee or customer surveys that ensure the autonomy and anonymity of participation necessary for honest and valuable feedback.

Chapter 14: Vision into Reality

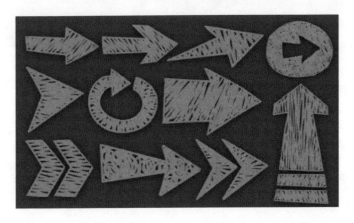

Here's What to Expect

- ✓ Summarise the expectations and takeaways of previous chapters
- ✓ Urge Executive Leaders to transform in the right way
- ✓ Introduce the authors as Trusted Advisors.

Transformation involves much more than a horizontal or vertical move. It refers to a fundamental and broad change. *The Leadership Shift* has sought to parse that change from multiple directions hoping it can support your move to a senior-level executive position or to a more significant role in a larger complex organisation.

Executive Leaders are burdened by multi-tasking, pulled in different directions by multiple distractions, and threatened by multiple risks. However, this is reductionist and oversimplified if you do not look further.

I have tried to examine executive leadership from a holistic view. There is a dynamic that informs, inspires, and challenges top executives. Successful leaders are fluid, flexible, adaptive, and agile. They are works-in-progress. Their transformation is constant rather than incremental. So, I tried to return regularly to that theme.

Theories, Tools, and Techniques

Chapter 1 reviewed the contemporary context in which Executive Leaders find themselves. The challenges vary with the nature and size of the organisation. They differ in various markets and according to the organisation's purpose.

These challenges are not singular or formulaic, so using templates to resolve them is inefficient and ineffective. Challenges may be foreseen, but they are also fluid and unpredictable. The complexity requires Executive Leaders who respond thoughtfully, decide prudently, and adapt readily.

In light of this, I examined how executives must:

- *Deal* with the recruitment, development, and retention of the talent needed to design and educate the organisation's future.

- *Form* productive relationships with all stakeholders—not just the shareholders.

- *Build* and trust high-performing teams willing to form strategic partnerships.

- *Focus* on opportunities instead of organisational pain points.

- *Discern* what needs changing rather than pursue their agenda.

- *Remove* barriers to success and provide employees with the tools and technologies that forestall problems.

- *Understand*, appreciate, empathise, and respect inside and outside stakeholders for their contributions to dialogue, collaboration, and innovation.

Chapter 2 analysed the Executive Leaders' crucial accountability for designing, structuring, and sustaining customer relationships. Executive accountability starts with a deep understanding that customers are people—complex decision makers. They are much more than data, and while they may produce revenue, they are much more than producers.

Commitment to customer satisfaction and respect for customer feedback starts at the top. Gathering data on customer behaviour is invaluable, but customer information lies somewhere in the data. That information holds clues to past, current, and future customer decisions. Executive Leaders will wade deep into the customer relationships and the departments and organisational functions that support them.

THE LEADERSHIP SHIFT

Executive Leaders are wise to build and integrate automated customer relationship management systems. However, automation is not the whole answer.

Effective Executive Leaders must:

- *Anticipate* customer input. They must lean forward and into the challenges posed by customers, strategically using feed-forward intelligence instead of leaving things to after-the-fact reporting.

- *Connect* with customers directly. Executive Leaders are encouraged to call customers regularly to survey their satisfaction, opinions, and recommendations.

- *Dig* deep into the data to find the personalities in the numbers, transactions, and demographics.

- *Improve* the status of Customer Service and other functions with customer contact.

- *Enable* and empower an organisational culture of customer respect and responsiveness with enough autonomy for employees to address customer concerns with agility.

- *Provide* customers with "win-win" options finding value in lessons learned from even their most negative feedback.

- *Invest* in multichannel customer access to secure the information needed to tailor the customer profile most suitable for their product or service. They build and sustain customer relationships by defining the customer with whom they want to work.

- *Develop* products and services consistent with core values important to the customers and communities within which they produce, perform, and profit.

- *Accent* the positive, leading with this optimism and constructive listening. Executive Leaders inspire and motivate with values, words, and actions.

- *Help* customers own their experience, offering customised relationships.

Chapter 3 reviewed the need for finding a Trusted Advisor. Given the pressure felt by Executive Leaders, the demand for their time and attention, and the need for their prompt and prudent decision-making, executives need advice on many individual tasks like labour law, taxation, workplace risk management, and more. However, they may need counselling to support personal development, organisational strategy, and agile execution.

Executives must develop relationships with advisors. There are many people in the consulting business, so you should shop well. You must research the recommended advisors, contact references, and order extensive background checks.

Advisors have access to confidential information, including marketing strategies, personnel records, and intellectual property. You want a fiduciary, an advisor who puts your interests first. The chosen advisor must excel at key metrics:

- Independent of other loyalties, the advisor must promise undivided attention to your organisation's critical needs.

- Trusted with the data and evidence necessary to shape opinions and sharpen decisions.

- Driven by constructive listening, able to lead conversations, take notes, and ask questions.

- Able to use respect and empathy to establish rapport with organisation stakeholders at all levels.

- Focused on partnership—serving and delivering—rather than directing and ordering.

Chapter 4 explored the phenomenon and threat in "decision fatigue." Executive Leaders make decisions; decisions are their primary task. However, the number and nature of the decisions can be physically and mentally exhausting. They must come to terms with decision fatigue to have any life-work balance of their own.

Fatigued Executive Leaders risk making hasty decisions. They may opt for shortcuts or form dangerous personal habits to avoid the pressures. The chapter urges senior executives to learn to discern what is essential and delegate, enable, and empower subordinates.

Successful Executive Leaders will:

- Adopt a positive and healthy life/work balance.

- Reduce the number of essential decisions.

- Build solid and capable teams with high potential leaders.

- Develop a collaborative culture where everyone respects agile *ad hoc* solutions.

- Embrace and model an optimistic behaviour that communicates confidence in their decisions.

Chapter 5 dealt with designing a proprietary competitive strategy. This highly competitive global economy tempts executive strategists to imitate or copy the approach of successful competitors. Imitative strategies can work. However, paying slavish attention to the competition takes focus away from growth and innovation's vital work.

A "*me-too*" mindset minimises your organisation's unique sales proposition. Its focus "on the other" takes attention away from *what* and *why* your organisation exists. The most admired and impactful leaders design and execute strategies of their OWN making.

Stakeholders rightly hold Executive Leaders accountable for the results, impacts, and benefits of well-developed and delivered strategies.

To make it original and effective, they must:

- **Articulate the strategy in clear and succinct language.**

  Executive Leaders must frame easily remembered and repeated mission and vision statements. The phrasing must become the north star for alignment of effort and purpose.

- **Picture the total customer and stakeholder experience.**

Leaders draw large and small pictures that connect and integrate plans, actions, and values. Their pictures emphasise the dynamic and fluid over the rational, incremental, and horizontal.

- **Leverage and optimise the talents of peers, colleagues, and junior managers.**

An emphasis on collaboration respects the diverse inputs of capable experts and specialists. They understand there is no value added in working alone, so they share work and seek counsel aligned with the strategic purpose.

- **Set pricing wisely.**

Organisations providing premium products and services can demand higher prices. Aiming for premium branding, you distinguish and differentiate your organisation strategically.

- **Identify your organisation's specific market.**

Chasing another organisation's market can be exhausting and counterproductive. At best, the chase will be imitative, static, and second best.

Chapter 6 introduced Agile thinking. Legacy organisations with military hierarchies have focused on projects and programs as frameworks for meeting objectives. These are straight-through processes where each step consumes the previous step's outputs until the product rolls out at the end of the process.

The legacy concept emphasises the procedural and functional. Performance becomes a matter of counting Key Performance Indicators (KPIs) for efficiency, economy, and effectiveness.

With this emphasis on Profit and Loss (P&L), their leaders undervalued the dynamic and fluid nature of an organisation's production.

Contemporary organisations, institutions, businesses, and others have chosen a more Agile path. Agile thinking and methodologies rely on cyclic reiterations of development, deployment, discernment, and improved design. This continuing improvement process requires a climate where autonomy and adhocracy are empowered.

Organisations develop Strategy Roadmaps that picture and share the strategic parameters to align efforts and impacts. A Strategy Roadmap begins with a clear statement of priorities. It illustrates the projected time frame and estimates the costs. Moreover, it indicates how stakeholder alignment will satisfy customer experience.

There is some challenge in designing, creating, and executing an effective Strategy Roadmap. It must integrate multiple paths to deliver incremental benefits at defined milestones. It takes mental agility to align all stakeholder interests, tasks, and behaviours with a clear understanding of its purpose.

Transitioning to Agile thinking and execution presents new challenging options for executives, especially those with little experience. However, with outside support, they can:

- *Align* individuals and teams to organisational purpose. They must invest stakeholders in mapping alignment from the top down and across the organisation.

- *Create* teams fitted to short- and long-term deliverables with team leaders known to embrace the organisation's vision entirely.

- *Empower* organisational people, practices, and processes to focus on fulfilling the customers' experience.

- *Enable* and empower a culture of psychological safety where mutual respect increases the emotional connectedness that makes everyone an invested stakeholder.

- *Draw* strategic roadmaps without barriers or potholes. They provide the tools and resources, training and support, and energy and passion for success.

- *Maximise* reciprocal communication with keywords and phrases that enable and add value to assessment, collaboration, dialogue, feedback, and stakeholder experience.

- *Ensure* autonomy for formal and informal Agile and ad hoc response and reiteration.

Chapter 7 offered a tentative look at leveraging technology for organisational purposes, "tentative" because the topic, terms, and tools advance so fast. It covers the broad aggregation and application of discipline, experience, and tools that directly and indirectly alter human experience.

Organisations rely on technology to accumulate and assess newly available and expanding data. They must support and manage market analysis and customer experience as well as sustain and scale results-based decision-making.

Innovation more than invention drives contemporary competition. Leading executives must not discount either, but they must differentiate between the concepts. Invention provides opportunity while innovation disrupts the norm. Executives also are urged to avoid technology that harms social and environmental ecosystems.

The acceleration of technology confronts executives with compelling demands to accept, adapt, and apply. Ignoring the pressures risks the loss of talent, productivity, and deliverables. They also risk choosing technology that fails to deliver an aligned customer experience.

To avoid missteps, Executive Leaders must move past considering Information Technology as a service function, a helpdesk available for repairs and networking. They must form strategic partnerships with the organisation's Information Technology team, expanding and valuing its strategic potential.

- Cybersecurity has become an organisational priority. Organisations must protect their intellectual property as well as their customer experience.

- Information Technology has become a vital key to the organisation's resilience in the face of local and global crises.

- Cloud applications are challenging, innovative, and necessary for any organisation's performance and continuity.

- Complex information systems weave through all an organisation's functions and plans, making them the key to full integration and alignment.

- Social media platforms offer a new opportunity and challenge for executives to lead or follow public opinion.

- Information is an asset needing management if an organisation is to process raw materials, deploy deliverables, manage currency, leverage human capital, and more.

- Corporate Governance and Risk Management (CGRM) increases the call for risk-taking and risk management.

- Organisations depend on complex hardware infrastructures providing information and internet access to multiple functions and across integrated functions.

- Optimised information systems process and provide the data executives need to comply with governance demands.

- Accelerating and emerging technology requires attention and assessment to move the organisation from the status quo to a sustainable competitive role.

Chapter 8 recognised the leaders' obligation to optimise their organisation's operations and culture. Traditionally, they have been champions of economy, efficiency, and effectiveness. Today, these must align with the organisation's stated goals and values. There is less focus on supply chains and more dedication to optimising the customer experience.

An optimised organisation resonates with a fluid and flexible dynamic. It pursues ideation and reiteration to maximise quality deliverables and the customers' journey. Executive Leaders will lead optimisation in their organisations by:

- *Using* digitisation to reduce overhead instead of cutting costs and labour burden.

- *Defining* clear Key Performance Indicators (KPIs) that assess performance as it contributes value to aligned organisational purpose.

- *Managing* risk to ensure workplace safety, agency compliance, and equity among stakeholders.

- *Redesigning* supply chains and increasing efficiencies as defined by purpose rather than profit.

- *Reimagining* the Information Technology discipline's function and focus to partner strategically on integrating systems and alignment with mission and vision.

- *Committing* to a digitised future that uses IT as a partner in lowering costs, improving processes, and empowering people.

Chapter 9 imagines the future of work. The nature of work has changed radically, and advancing technology continues to impact work and workers heavily. They have been left confused and overwhelmed, unable to tell an opportunity from a problem.

Technology has shrunk the world. The internet has made vast information available to all, but the volume also includes mis- and dis-information. People everywhere can learn procedures new to them, yet the lack of resources frustrates many of them. Most people do not comprehend the Algorithms, Analytics, Artificial Intelligence, Cloud Computing, and more that already inform their lives, so they are threatened by anything new.

Executive Leaders, then, must make engaging work possible by:

- *Designing* work that attracts, engages, and retains workers.
- *Cocreating* a culture of connectedness and collaboration.
- *Recruiting* for talent—not just hands and feet—because all work will require new skill sets.
- *Shape* work in the context of cybercrime and pandemic disease.
- *Reimagine* work as project-based rather than task-based.
- *Train* and development management fit to inspire and motivate.

Chapter 10 introduced the omnichannel customer experience. Today's Executive Leaders have been coming to terms with multiple social media platforms. They appreciate the potential for reaching deep into markets. Still, they must defend against negative reviews.

Omnichannel capability requires the integration and optimisation of all the channels available. The internet eliminates the customers' physical shopping experience, so provider organisations must create an alternative to the tactile experience.

Omnichannel marketing makes products available in many ways across all devices. Customers can engage with the shops and products on smartphones, smart televisions, tablets, and personal computers. They enable chatting, sizing, colouring, customizing, and more.

Omnichannel technology also integrates customer connections with strategic responses in marketing, operations, customer service, shipping and handling, and supply chain logistics. The technology collects data on customer profiles, demographics, and shopping behaviours regarding the time of day, season, price margins, and much more.

The omnichannel experience requires Executive Leaders to:

- *Map* the customer experience with enough detail to add texture, context, and tangibility to shopping.

- *Differentiate* between customer wants and needs—as communicated on multiple social media outlets—to serve them better.

- *Fit* the customer's profile as determined by prior and evolving research.

- *Engaging* shoppers to access the organisation's website, spend some time there, and then buy.

- *Optimise* marketing with digital tools that communicate brand and product in multiple ways on various venues.

- *Secure* customer loyalty as the most efficient way to grow and sustain sales.

Chapter 11 found it crucial to build and sustain strong stakeholder relationships. It differentiated stakeholders from shareholders. Top executives must deal directly with their shareholders owing them, as they do, a return on their investment.

However, today's organisations take a more holistic approach, seeking to produce value for all those interested in their performance, outcomes, and impacts. If organisations are to transform from an emphasis on outputs to outcomes, they must respect everyone's roles, including the producers and customers.

Stakeholders include suppliers, senior and junior managers, employees, business partners, customers, and consultants. Anyone who touches productivity or executes strategy to create deliverables is a stakeholder.

- Building solid relationships consumes a large part of Executive Leaders' lives, energy, and emotion. So, they should identify the priorities relevant to stakeholder groups and subgroups.

- Stakeholder interests change and evolve. So, Executive Leaders must delegate relationships built on functional expertise, personal interest, and shared values.

- It is not enough to engage stakeholders; they expect satisfaction. Executive Leaders cannot manage all those expectations, but they can focus on systems that align wants and needs to the organisation's avowed purpose and values.

- Global communication has given virtual stakeholders a stronger voice. Executive Leaders, then, are challenged to create virtual relationships. Working on internet-enabled meeting platforms like Zoom reduces the in-person social connection and requires new skills to keep participants engaged.

- Social relationships struggle to survive in a climate of future shock. Executive Leaders, therefore, must take the lead in creating a consistent, optimistic work environment where mutual respect drives engagement, energy, and excitement.

Chapter 13 studied the structure and influence of a healthy organisational culture. It defined "culture" as a spirit that informs a social body and reveals itself in signs, symbols, songs, and other consistent behaviours.

It may follow one, more, or a combination of modes that range from a coercive bureaucracy of command and control to an enabling bureaucracy of agile creativity. Healthy organisations make things happen. They change markets, satisfy customers, engage stakeholders, and more.

Influential Executive Leaders will lead purposeful organisations if they expect to realise their purpose. Such organisations are distinguished by:

- A robust website asserts the organisation's mission and vision and links to the people and processes that deliver the promise.

- High employee retention stabilises and sustains the talent needed to make a difference.

- As lived and modelled by the executive leadership, systemic trust enables and empowers creative and innovative collaboration.

- Organisation members enjoy a community, a tangible camaraderie engaged in work.

- The organisation values quality over quantity; productivity is measured by good work rather than fast work.

- Work is a seamless extension of people's lives with little need for maintaining a life/work balance.

- Organisations understand their role as one system in a community of social and ecological networks.

- Organisation members benefit from equitable and just compensation commensurate with their contribution and needs.

- Customers benefit from relationships that show respect for their wants and needs.

- Social media readily share customer and worker reviews of their organisation convenience.

Make It Happen

The Leadership Shift was prepared for several audiences who find themselves in transition. For instance, in their passion to get started, entrepreneurs sometimes forget that their future depends on the steps they take at the beginning.

Other organisations are undergoing transformation themselves, and their executives must make crucial decisions rather than go along for the ride. Some readers are on a career path that trains and develops their high potential for executive-level positions. Some executives are moving into new roles in their respective organisations or executive positions at new organisations. All these people are in transition.

The book has confronted the challenges facing executives, and it has scrutinised those challenges as contexts for personal and organisational transformation. Hopefully, it has proposed solutions to ease the transition.

However, one consistent theme has been that even high-potential executives cannot succeed alone. They need the support of Trusted Advisors who are experienced and equipped to:

- *Ease* burdensome, time-intensive, and exhausting projects.

- *Share* assessment, analysis, and accountability for short- and long-term projects.

- *Profile* executive team members, team leaders, and managers.

- *Design* and launch initiatives creating frameworks for organisational expansion, marketing and branding, enhanced employee engagement, and optimised risk management.

- *Customise* strategic technology applications and capabilities.

About the Author

Stuart Andrews is a Trusted Advisor and a Forbes Coaches Council Member specialising in corporate restructuring and transformation. He has extensive experience designing and implementing large-scale transformation programs. He has served in interim executive leadership roles while also acting as a Senior Advisor to management teams and directors' boards.

Stuart develops partnerships with executives struggling with growth strategy, process optimisation, supply chain, contact centre customer service, and product development. He helps them find the right levers to drive improvement and transformation across Procurement, Finance, Human Resources, Legal, Operations, Marketing and Sales, and Research and Development. Stuart ensures that support services truly meet business needs as clients foster a culture of continuous innovation and growth that allows them to outpace competitors.

The Leadership Shift provides thought leadership on the ways and means to resolve the challenges faced by today's Executive Leaders. If you would like to discuss further or book a Free Discovery Session, please contact me via LinkedIn using the QR code below.

Works Cited

Chapter 1

Age and Tenure: Large-Cap vs. Small-Cap Board Comparisons. (2017, May 15). Retrieved from Equilar: https://www.equilar.com/blogs/258-age-and-tenure-large-cap-vs-small-cap-board.html

CEO Benchmarking Report. (2019, March 13). Retrieved from The Predictive Index: https://resources.predictiveindex.com/ebook/ceo-benchmarking-report-2019/

Emmons, J. (2019, April 12). *What's keeping CEOs up at night?* Retrieved from Guild: https://guild.co/blog/whats-keeping-ceos-up-at-night/

Kissel, N., & Foley, P. (2019, January 23). The 3 Challenges Every New CEO Faces. *Harvard Business Review.* Retrieved from https://hbr.org/2019/01/the-3-challenges-every-new-ceo-faces

Llopis, G. (2012, July 17). *Great Management Boils Down to One Major Thing.* Retrieved from Forbes.com: https://www.forbes.com/sites/glennllopis/2012/07/17/great-management-boils-down-to-one-major-thing/#471ea5a92204

Marcec, D. (2018, February 12). *CEO Tenure Rates.* Retrieved from Harvard Law School on Corporate Governance: https://corpgov.law.harvard.edu/2018/02/12/ceo-tenure-rates/

Thomas, B. (2019, January 19). *3 priorities for CEOs in 2019.* Retrieved from Webforum.com: https://www.weforum.org/agenda/2019/01/ceo-priorities-for-success-in-2019/

Welcome to the crisis era. Are you ready? CEO pulse on crisis. (2017). Retrieved from PWC.Global: https://www.pwc.com/gx/en/ceo-agenda/pulse/crisis.html

Chapter 2

Barroca, L., Dingsøyr, T., & Mikalsen, M. (2019). Agile Transformation: A Summary and Research Agenda from the First International Workshop. In R. Hoda (Ed.), *International Conference on Agile Software Development. 364.* Springer Natural, Cham, AG. Retrieved from https://link.springer.com/chapter/10.1007/978-3-030-30126-2_1

Ben Wu, J., Lin, I.-J., & Yang, M.-H. (2009). The Impact of a Customer Profile and Customer Participation on Customer Relation Management. *International Journal of Electronic Business Management, 7*(1), 57-69. Retrieved from https://link.springer.com/chapter/10.1007/978-3-030-30126-2_1

Bensemana, L. (2007, March 6). System and method for creating a true customer profile. Retrieved from https://patentimages.storage.googleapis.com/58/36/b8/594677736b9f1d/US7188076.pdf

Denning, S. (2019). Explaining Agile. Retrieved from http://blogs.forbes.com/stevedenning/.

Mulqueen, T. (2018, January 17). *How to Make the Most of Customer Insights.* Retrieved from Forbes.com: https://www.forbes.com/sites/tinamulqueen/2018/01/17/how-to-make-the-most-of-customer-insights/#51537eb21f85

Richardson, A. (2010, October 28). *Understanding Customer Experience.* Retrieved from Harvard Business Review: https://hbr.org/2010/10/understanding-customer-experie

The Path to Personalization. (2020). Retrieved from Forbes: https://www.forbes.com/sites/insights-treasuredata/2019/05/01/the-path-to-personalization/#652d802e7a76

Chapter 3

Bootcamp. XP Agile Universe Conference. Calgary, Alberta, Canada.

Hodgetts, P. (2004, August 15). Agile Planning, Tracking, and Project Manager

Paquette, P., & Frankl, M. (2016). *Agile Project Management for Business Transformation Success.* New York, NY: Business Expert Press.

Pruitt, J. (2017, June 14). *3 Top Traits of Effective Agile Leaders.* Retrieved from Inc.com: https://www.inc.com/jeff-pruitt/3-ways-to-leverage-agile-leadership.html

The Trusted Advisor Relationship. (2020). Retrieved from AESC.org: https://www.aesc.org/insights/magazine/article/trusted-advisor-relationship

Chapter 4

Baumeister, R., Bratslavsky, E., Muraven, M., & Tice, D. (1998). Ego Depletion: Is the Active Self a Limited Resource? (V. 7.-1. 1998, Ed.) *Journal of Personality and Social Psychology, 74*(5), 1252-1265. Retrieved from https://faculty.washington.edu/jdb/345/345%20Articles/Baumeister%20et%20al.%20(1998).pdf

Brousseau, K., Driver, M., Hourihan, G., & Larsson, R. (2006, February). The Seasoned Executive's Decision-Making Style. *Harvard Business Review.* Retrieved from Harvard Business Review.com

Tierney, J. (2011, August 17). *Do You Suffer from Decision Fatigue?* Retrieved from The New York Times Magazine: https://www.nytimes.com/2011/08/21/magazine/do-you-suffer-from-decision-fatigue.html

Chapter 5

Kim, W., & Mauborgne, R. (2015, March). Red Ocean Traps. *Harvard Business Review.* Retrieved from https://hbr.org/2015/03/red-ocean-traps

Reddy, N. (2018, February 12). *Want A Successful Business? Build an Effective Strategy.* Retrieved from Forbes: https://www.forbes.com/sites/forbescoachescouncil/2018/02/12/want-a-successful-business-build-an-effective-strategy/#4ce9ec8469bf

Chapter 6

Beheshti, N. (2019, January 16). *10 Timely Statistics About the Connection Between Employee Engagement and Wellness.* Retrieved from Forbes: https://www.forbes.com/sites/nazbeheshti/2019/01/16/10-timely-statistics-about-the-connection-between-employee-engagement-and-wellness/#2e32ce1a22a0

Linger, K. (2015, October 10). *Benefits – a necessity to deliver business value and a culture change but how do we achieve them?* Retrieved from Project Management Institute: https://www.pmi.org/learning/library/guidelines-successful-benefits-realization-9909

Lyons, R. (2017, July 10). *Feedback: You Need to Lead It.* Retrieved from Forbes: https://www.forbes.com/sites/richlyons/2017/07/10/feedback-you-need-to-lead-it/#78db6ba34a35

Mautin, T. (2014). *The Aligned Organization.* Paris: McKinsey & Company. Retrieved from https://www.mckinsey.com/~/media/McKinsey/Business%20Functions/Operations/Our%20Insights/The%20lean%20management%20enterprise/The%20aligned%20organization.ashx

Chapter 7

Augustyn, A. (2018, March 18). Technology. Retrieved from Encyclopedia Britannica https://www.britannica.com/technology/technology

Das, S. (2019, November 19). *Leveraging technology for better business productivity.* Retrieved from ET: CIO: https://cio.economictimes.indiatimes.com/news/strategy-and-management/leveraging-technology-for-better-business-productivity/72287307

Duval, D. (2019, January 28). *Today's Companies Have A Technology Adoption Problem, Not an Innovation Problem.* Retrieved from Forbes: https://www.forbes.com/sites/forbesnonprofitcouncil/2019/01/28/todays-companies-have-a-technology-adoption-problem-not-an-innovation-problem/#5111b2ca1f66

Greenwald, M. (2014, March 12). *What Exactly Is Innovation?* Retrieved from Forbes: https://www.forbes.com/sites/michellegreenwald/2014/03/12/what-exactly-is-innovation/#6d2862785e5a

Invention. (2020). Retrieved from Entrepreneur: https://www.entrepreneur.com/encyclopedia/invention

OECD. (2014). *Risk Management and Corporate Governance.* Governance. Paris: OECD Publishing. hps://doi.org/10.1787/9789264208636-en.

Otero, M. (2019, November 20). *3 Innovation Strategies for the Age of Digital Disruption.* Retrieved from Harvard Business Review: https://hbr.org/sponsored/2019/11/3-innovation-strategies-for-the-age-of-digital-disruption

Todhunter, J. (2009, April 22). *Defining Innovation.* Retrieved from FastCompany: https://www.fastcompany.com/1273187/defining-inno

Chapter 8

Arnold, R., & Wade, J. (2015, December). A Definition of Systems Thinking: A Systems Approach. *Procedia Computer Science.* doi: 10.1016/j.procs.2015.03.050

Barstow, S. (2019, February 12). *Ideal Overhead Percentage.* Retrieved from SmallBusiness.Chron.com: https://smallbusiness.chron.com/ideal-overhead-percentage-75876.html

Dam, R., & Teo, Y. (2020, April). *What is Design Thinking and Why Is It So Popular?* Retrieved from Interaction Design Foundation: https://www.interaction-design.org/literature/article/what-is-design-thinking-and-why-is-it-so-popular

Denning, S. (2017, October 15). *What Is Agile? The Four Essential Elements.* Retrieved from Forbes: https://www.forbes.com/sites/stevedenning/2017/10/15/what-is-agile-the-four-essential-elements/#5d511b956e85

Digitisation is helping to deliver goods faster. (2019, July 11). Retrieved from Economist: https://www.economist.com/special-report/2019/07/11/digitisation-is-helping-to-deliver-goods-faster

Hutcherson, R. (2014). *Organizational Optimization.* U.S.: AuthorHouse.

Kotter, P. (2012, November). *Accelerate!* Retrieved from Harvard Business Review: https://hbr.org/2012/11/accelerate

Introduction to the performance management cycle. (2014, November 21). Retrieved from AIG Group: https://www.aigroup.com.au/resourcecentre/hr/managing-performance/performance-management-cycle/introduction-to-the-performance-management-cycle/

Li, A. (n.d.). *What Is the Organizational-Efficiency Factor?* Retrieved from SmallBusiness.Chron: https://smallbusiness.chron.com/organizationalefficiency-factor-37839.html

Neuman, J. (1975, May). *Make Overhead Cuts That Last.* Retrieved from Harvard Business Review: https://hbr.org/1975/05/make-overhead-cuts-that-last

New book teaches business leaders how to harness the power of digital transformation for their organization. (2020, February 11). Bridgetown, NJ. Retrieved from http://web.a.ebscohost.com/ehost/detail/detail?vid=4&sid=24c1ca43-21e8-4bcf-8145-39f6eff3066c%40sdc-v-sessmgr01&bdata=JnNpdGU9ZWhvc3QtbGl2ZQ%3d%3d#AN=202002110900PR.NEWS.USPR.UN15428&db=bwh

Overby, S. (2017, November 6). *What is outsourcing? Definitions, best practices, challenges, and advice.* Retrieved from CIO: https://www.cio.com/article/2439495/outsourcing-outsourcing-definition-and-solutions.html

Chapter 9

Brett, C. (2018, October 15). *Blockchain disadvantages: 10 possible reasons not to enthuse.* Retrieved from Enterprise Times: https://www.enterprisetimes.co.uk/2018/10/15/blockchain-disadvantages-10-possible-reasons-not-to-enthuse/

Butler, E. (2020). *About Adam Smith.* Retrieved from Adam Smith Institute: https://www.adamsmith.org/about-adam-smith

Goggin, G., Vroman, A., Weatherall, K., Martin, F., & Sunman, L. (2019, March 31). Data and digital rights: recent Australian developments. *Internet Policy Review, 8*(1). doi:10.14763/2019.1.1390

McGregor, l., & Doshi, N. (2020, April 9). *How to Keep Your Team Motivated, Remotely.* Retrieved from Harvard Business Review: https://hbr.org/2020/04/how-to-keep-your-team-motivated-remotely

Mills, J., & Jan, C. (2017). The Gig Economy. APSCO Australia.

Reiff, N. (2020, February 1). *Blockchain Explained.* Retrieved from Investopedia: https://www.investopedia.com/terms/b/blockchain.asp

Revealing the True Size of Australia's Gig Workforce. (2019, June 18). Retrieved from Delivering for all Victorians: https://www.premier.vic.gov.au/revealing-the-true-size-of-australia's-gig-workforce/

Chapter 10

Ang, L., & Buttle, F. (n.d.). ROI on CRM: a customer-journey approach. Macquarie Graduate School of Management.

Denning, S. (2011, April 1). *Is Delighting the Customer Profitable?* Retrieved from Forbes: https://www.forbes.com/sites/stevedenning/2011/04/01/is-delighting-the-customer-profitable/#22595c16e874

Duncan, E., Fanderl, H., Marchler, N., & Neher, K. (2016, Winter). Customer Experience: creating value through transforming customer journeys. McKinsey & Company.

Ehrlichman, M. (2014, November 14). *The 8 Principles of Customer Delight.* Retrieved from Inc.: https://www.inc.com/matt-ehrlichman/the-8-principles-of-customer-delight.html

Gammeri, S., & Breschi, R. (2017). *The CEO Guide to Customer Experience.* McKinsey & Company.

Hennick, C. (2019, September 12). *Retailers Ramp Up Investments in Omnichannel.* Retrieved from BizTech: https://biztechmagazine.com/article/2019/09/retailers-ramp-investments-omnichannel

Channel 11

Enright, S., McElrath, R., & Taylor, A. (2016, October). The Future of Stakeholder Engagement. BSR. Retrieved from https://www.bsr.org/reports/BSR_Future_of_Stakeholder_Engagement_Report.pdf

Freeman, R. (2010). *Strategic Management: A Stakeholder Approach.* Cambridge, UK: Cambridge University Press.

Freeman, R., & McVea, J. (2001, January 1). A Stakeholder Approach to Strategic Management. *SSRN Electronic Journal.*

Kimiagari, S., Keivanpour, S., Mohiuddin, M., & Van Horne, C. (2013, October 15). The Cooperation Complexity Rainbow: Challenges of Stakeholder Involvement in Managing Multinational Firms. *International Journal of Business and Management, 8*(22). Retrieved from http://dx.doi.org/10.5539/ijbm.v8n22p50

Shareholder Theory. (n.d.). Retrieved from CEOpedia Management Online: https://ceopedia.org/index.php/Shareholder_theory

Chapter 12

Abbot, L., Batty, R., & Bevegni, S. (2016). Global Recruiting Trends 2016. LinkedIn Talent Solutions. Retrieved from https://business.linkedin.com/content/dam/business/talent-solutions/global/en_us/c/pdfs/GRT16_GlobalRecruiting_100815.pdf

Albrecht, W. (2016, May 20). Why Good Corporate Governance is So Important. *BYU Wheatley Institution*. Retrieved from https://wheatley.byu.edu/why-good-corporate-governance-is-so-important

Arora, C., Caitlin, T., Forrest, W., Kaplan, J., & Vinter, L. (2020, August). The New Normal: The recovery will be digital. McKinsey & Company.

Australia. (2019). Retrieved from Transparency International: https://www.transparency.org/en/countries/australia#

Broderick, S. & Witte, I. (2018). Digital Transformation: How Advanced Technologies are impacting financial reporting and auditing. KPGM International. Retrieved from https://home.kpmg/content/dam/kpmg/us/pdf/2018/02/us-jnet-2018-issue1-2-KPMG-Forbes-Digital-Transformation-report.PDF

Cooke-Davies, T., Crawford, L., Hobbs, J. B., Labuschagne, L., & Remington, K. (2006, July 19). *Exploring the role of the executive sponsor.* Retrieved from PMI: https://www.pmi.org/learning/library/role-executive-sponsor-support-investments-8096

Durugboa, C., Tiwarib, A., & Alcock, J. (2013, June). Modelling information flow for organisations: A review of approaches and future challenges. *International Journal of Information Management, 33*(3), 597-610. Retrieved from https://www.sciencedirect.com/science/article/abs/pii/S0268401213000121

Eccles, B. (2016, January 12). Why Is Good Governance Important? *Forbes*. Retrieved from https://www.forbes.com/sites/bobeccles/2016/01/12/why-is-good-governance-important/#4e9449985750

Ethics, morality, law – what's the difference? (2016, September 27). Retrieved from The Ethics Centre: https://ethics.org.au/ethics-morality-law-whats-the-difference/

Evaluation and Value for Money. (2017, November). Retrieved from Australian Government: Australian Institute of Family Services: https://aifs.gov.au/cfca/publications/evaluation-and-value-money#:~:text=What%20is%20Value%20for%20Money,an%20intervention %20represents%20good%20value.

Governance, Management and the Role of the Board of Directors. (2009, May). *NGC Connect e-NEWs*. Retrieved from https://www.inphilanthropy.org/sites/default/files/resources/Crucial%20Diffe rence%20Between%20Governance%20%26%20Management-AKT%20LLP-2011.pdf

Knaus, C. (2020, January 23). *Australia among 21 nations where perceived corruption has worsened.* Retrieved from The Guardian: https://www.theguardian.com/australia-news/2020/jan/23/australia-among-21-nations-where-perceived-corruption-has-worsened

Miller, J. (2017, October 17). *What is a project management office (PMO) and do you need one?* Retrieved from CIO: https://www.cio.com/article/2441862/what-is-a-project-management-office-pmo-and-do-you-need-one.html

Mitchell, R. (2009). The Crucial Difference between Governance and Management. AKT LLP.

Vega, S. (2019, December). Keeping Us Up Late at Night: the big issues facing business leaders in 2020. KPMG International. Retrieved from: https://assets.kpmg/content/dam/kpmg/au/pdf/2019/issues-facing-australian-leaders-2020-outlook.pdf

Chapter 13

Brunetto, Y., Teo, S., Shacklock, K., & Farr-Wharton, F. (2012). Emotional intelligence, job satisfaction, well-being and engagement: explaining organisational commitment and turnover intentions in policing. Human Resource Management Journal, Vol 22, no 4, 2012, pages 428–441.

Carter, L. (2010). In Great Company. New York: McGraw-Hill.

Chamorro-Premuzic, T., Garrad, L., & and Elzinga, E. (2018, November 28). Is Employee Engagement Just a Reflection of Personality? Retrieved from Harvard Business Review: https://hbr.org/2018/11/is-employee-engagement-just-a-reflection-of-personality

Cohn, A. (2018, April 9). The Best Practice Institute Thinks Workplaces Should Be 'Emotionally Connected.' Forbes. Retrieved from https://www.forbes.com/sites/alisacohn/2018/04/09/the-best-practice-institute-thinks-workplaces-should-be-emotionally-connected/#6ec436927f39

Csikszentmihalyi, M. (1991). Flow: The Psychology of Optimal Experience. New York: Harper-Collins.

Kittredge, A. (2010, Spring). Predicting Work and Organizational Engagement with Work and Personal Factors. San Jose State University: Scholar Works. Retrieved from

https://scholarworks.sjsu.edu/cgi/viewcontent.cgi?referer=https://scholar.goo
gle.com/&httpsredir=1&article=4767&context=etd_theses

Mahon, E., Taylor, S., & Boyatzis, R. (2004, November 18). Antecedents of organizational engagement: exploring vision, mood, and perceived organizational support with emotional intelligence as a moderator. Frontiers in Psychology. Retrieved from https://www.frontiersin.org/articles/10.3389/fpsyg.2014.01322/full#B7

O'Driscoll, M., & Randall, D. (1999). Perceived Organisational Support, Satisfaction with Rewards, and Employee Job Involvement and Organisational Commitment. Applied Psychology: An International Review, 48, 2, 197-202.

Ryan, L. (2018, May 19). Ten Unmistakable Signs of a Healthy Workplace. Retrieved from Forbes: https://www.forbes.com/sites/lizryan/2018/05/19/ten-unmistakable-signs-of-a-healthy-workplace/#55c87a0f5cad

Tabrizi, B., Lam, E., Girard, K., & Irvin, V. (2019 March 13). Digital Transformation is Not About Technology. Retrieved from HBR.com: https://hbr.org/2019/03/digital-transformation-is-not-about-technology

Tharp, B. (2009, April). Four Organizational Culture Types. Haworth. Retrieved from https://pdfs.semanticscholar.org/b0e2/fd342fcf402920e264f15070276b79be1e25.pdf

The Engaged Workplace. (2020). Retrieved from Gallop: https://www.gallup.com/services/190118/engagedworkplace.aspx

Volo, K. (2014, August 8). 5 Cultural Keys to Employee Engagement. The HR Observer. Retrieved from https://www.thehrobserver.com/5-cultural-keys-to-employee-engagement/

Watkins, M. (2013, March 15). What is organizational culture? And why should we care? Harvard Business Review. Retrieved from https://hbr.org/2013/05/what-is-organizational-culture

Zimmerman, K. (2017, July 13). What is Culture? Retrieved from LiveScience: https://www.livescience.com/21478-what-is-culture-definition-of-culture.html

INDEX

Made in United States
Orlando, FL
15 May 2022

17903660R00167